Wholeness:
The Universe
Within

Poetry and Philosophy
Inspired by Loving Awareness

By: Maddie Rekowski

Just like the moon, you are always whole.

Even if parts of you cannot be seen all
the time,

all you need is a little light to find them.

Acknowledgments

Infinite hours of meditation and lessons from spiritual leaders have gone into the making of this book. Every single person to have ever crossed my path or touched my life through the invisible string is the inspiration for these poems and excerpts. These philosophical concepts can be attributed to lessons from the Tao Te Ching, the Bhagavad Gita, Toltec wisdom, countless Eastern philosophers and many spiritual leaders including Buhdda, Ram Dass, Maharaj-ji, Alan Watts, Deepak Chopra, Dalai Lama, and most of all humanity. The words of these leaders are like the seeds that have been used to plant this book. This book would be nothing without the knowledge from world-renowned teachings and ancient philosophies. Let my unique interpretation of this wisdom take you into loving awareness that has always been within us.

I also want to extend my gratitude to my mom, Kimberly Rekowski, who helped me edit, format, and publish this book. As a self-published children's book author herself, she taught me lots of valuable information. Mom, without your support I would not be the person I am today in any way. You make the world go around.

This book full of poetry and art is dedicated to every living thing on earth. May we all benefit from the words that promote peace and love like the gift that keeps on giving. May every being feel the love they are composed of.

Table of Contents

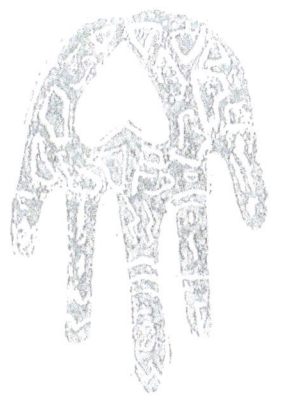

This book is not a race to the end.

There is no prize for the person who finishes the fastest.

The only prize is what you get out of it by applying your heart and your mind.

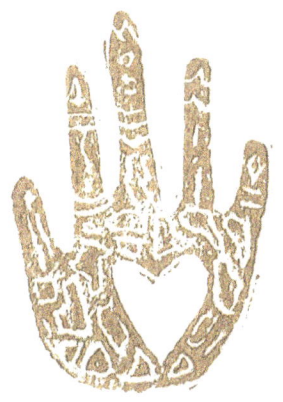

Introduction

There is more to you than you could ever understand. You are more than life. You are more than a body or a brain. You are more than your thoughts; you are more than your name. You are beyond good and bad, right and wrong. You are the energy that has never been created and can never be destroyed. You are the wind that howls through every human life, through birth, and through death. You are all the emotions wrapped up in a beautiful, mortal life. You are the tears of joy and the tears of pain.

What you are can not be confined in the limits of words or concepts. You are the creator and the created, the lover and the beloved. You are the quietness of the loving awareness behind your thoughts. You are everything and nothing at all.

In all beings there is a place where only love exists. This comes from the realization that we are one, one consciousness, one love. The same me that's writing this is the same you that's reading this. When you travel past the mind, past the body, that is where we meet, in love. What is consciousness and how can we tap into it? If you notice that someone has really big hands, you receive a thought that says, "that person has really big hands." Your consciousness will observe that thought. Consciousness is not the thought, rather the awareness of that thought. Most people identify with what they think because they believe that they are the ones thinking. You are not the thinker; you are the observer.

Consciousness delves between opinion and fact. It is beyond right and wrong. It is an awareness of what is; it is the ultimate truth. The loving awareness that constructs consciousness comes from the unconditional acceptance of what is, without judgment or subjectivity.

You can notice your consciousness whenever you simply observe whatever is happening in the present moment. The place where you watch your thoughts go by is a place where only bliss and love reside. We all have this same place of loving awareness within us. It is what created and perceives everything that exists today. That is why we are not separate. We are awareness. It does not matter where you come from, what religion you practice, what gender you are, what you believe in, we all have the same awareness. The observation of life is through the same higher power that is manifested through each of our human bodies.

In this world, love operates through many disguises. Your body is a disguise for who you really are. When you look down at your hands, you see separateness. You think that those hands belong to you and only you. The illusion is that every human believes their hands are their own, but the awareness behind that belief is all the same. It is all the same consciousness. Your hands are no more your hands than they are your neighbors.

The disguises we are given to operate on this physical plane come with an ego. Your ego is who you think you are: your name, your body, your blood, and your emotions.

Definition - Ego /'ēgō/

A figment of the mind that identifies with a personal, separate self from the world around.

When you look in the mirror, your ego says, "That's me!" Or maybe it says, "That's me..." with a melancholic tone. Your ego makes you believe that you are separate from the nature, people, and objects around you. If I told you that your individuality was an illusion, your ego would set off alarms in your brain begging you not to forget about it. It is safe to say that your ego wants to be special. Actually, your ego just wants things in general. It wants because it feels that there is a lack. The ego makes oneself feel incomplete or flawed. This is what leads to desire, shame, greed, and suffering.

Although being attached to the ego causes suffering, being opposed to having an ego is just another attachment to the idea of a life without an ego. The only way to work around this egotistical dance is to accept all that is. Accept the dualism between the polarities of the world. You are a human, but you are also the universe. You experience anger and sadness, but you also experience joy and laughter. The dark and light coexist; one cannot exist without the other. Beauty is only found in wholeness. **Life is not about being a holy spirit; it is about being whole.** Love is letting things be the way they are and making space for all that exists. The beauty that is within you is only there because of everything that works to create the magnificent being you are.

There are no parts of yourself that are wrong to love. There are no parts of the world that are wrong to love. Life becomes much more fulfilling and joyous once you learn to relish the feeling of being a human rather than fighting it.

In this life, you only get one body and one heart to live through. Having a heart means experiencing pain, but it also means experiencing love. This book is meant to open your eyes to love that already is within yourself and always has been. It is to remind yourself that you are perfect in this moment and for eternity.

Your life does not have to be a battle between your human traits and your spiritual being. All that exists is perfect. Your wholeness is what makes it all so beautiful. Life is about waking up to the loving consciousness that you are while also honoring your incarnation.

Not all will understand.

But those who do,

don't need to be understood.

Faith is not about trusting in something bigger than yourself.

It is about trusting something within yourself that you can't always see.

The Self

Life is very interesting because we are given one incarnation to have as our identity, to control, and to take care of. You wake up every morning with yourself, eat every meal with yourself, meet new people with yourself, experience all of your happiest and saddest moments with yourself. And every night, when your head hits your pillow, you close your own eyes and fall asleep with yourself. You spend every moment being yourself from the time you popped out of your mothers womb all the way to the time that your-self dies.

We spend 24 hours a day for 80+ years with this idea of who we are. In the grand scheme of the universe, that is only a blink of time, but we as humans know how long life feels. Life can feel like a prison sentence because we are trapped in these mortal, limited bodies. We are given a name, a family, a home, and we are confined by the walls of our skin. It feels like we have no choice in what body we end up in because we forget that our consciousness created this entire experience. Even if you think that the body you landed in was all due to chance or if you believe in divine purpose, you are here in this body and there's nothing you can do about it. It is not your choice to be who you are, but it is your path. You must decide if you want to resist your path or accept and love it as it is. This includes loving who you are with all your baggage and your human imperfections.

Having to spend an entire lifetime with a person that you hate and are always rejecting would be miserable, yet so many people do it with themselves. Many people wake up everyday in a body that feels like a heavy, unbearable weight. They look in the mirror, see all of their failures and walk around with shame eating away at their heart. I think most people can admit that there are times where we treat ourselves with the most ruthless and unforgiving malice. This is not because we are unlovable as people; it is because we were taught that we were unlovable by other people who don't know how to love. **All the hate that you have acquired for yourself is not natural.** It is something that has been instilled in you just like any other form of hate such as racism or homophobia. You are not born hating yourself. The good thing about what we have been taught is that we can always reverse it with conscious thinking. To learn to love all the parts of who you are, you must cultivate an intimate relationship between your ego and your eternal spirit.

The relationship between the spirit and the ego is one of a parent and a child. Your ego is like a child that doesn't yet have the capacity to understand it all. Your human brain needs concepts to function because it was built that way. It will never fully grasp infinity of your being because your ego is limited for a reason. Your ego feels small and separate, confused and weary. Your ego naturally has limitations that don't allow you to zoom out of your myopic perspective and see the oneness of it all. Things tend to appear more confusing the closer you get to it. You as a person are

20

experiencing the world through a microscope. You do not have the ability to see the whole picture of the unity of the universe through human eyes. There is no question why you find the idea existence daunting and unruly, just as a child does.

Your eternal spirit is like the parent who watches the ego grow and learn to exist on this physical plane. Your eternal spirit never leaves your side because its role is to support you through your entire journey. It loves you unconditionally just like any parent loves their child. Your eternal spirit does not care about the color of your skin or the amount of fat you have on your bones. It does not care if people would describe you as kind or callous. The eternal spirit knows that your-self is just a manifestation of itself in human form.

The spirit is always there for you if you are willing to listen. If you get really quiet in the mind and let your body relax, you can hear your spirit saying, "I love you. Everything is okay." Lots of people find this spirit through meditation. Some even find it through poetry or music. Although there are many useful tools to get connected with the eternal spirit, they all lead to the same place of unconditional love.

Take a moment to feel this divine support that has always been with you. Relax your eyes and feel that knowing that you are just doing everything right, regardless of how it may feel on the human level. This peace is just a deeper version of you without form, without thought.

The spirit and the ego are always connected. The ego is an illusion because it is just the spirit in disguise. A great spiritual teacher, Ram Dass, compared our egos to a spacesuit. This spacesuit is necessary for us to operate on the human level but within the spacesuit is the eternal spirit.

Some people believe in killing the ego because it is the root of suffering and separateness, but killing the ego is a rejection of what you've been given by the universe. A rejection of anything is another way to disconnect from being everything. Your ego is a gift from your highest self saying, "Here you go! Experience the complexity of human existence. Take this amazing journey with a beautiful human body. Feel all that your human heart can bear: laugh, cry, sing, and dance, then find me once you're ready to be one with it all."

Your ego is no less the spirit than the spirit is the spirit. That is why it is so important for you to cultivate an intimate relationship with yourself. Treat your darkness with grace and compassion as any parent should do with their child. You have a childhood, honor that. You have a family, honor that. Get to a place where you can simultaneously be a daughter, or a son, or a mother, or a father while also being the universe. You do not have to choose a side. Non-duality is the realization that there is nothing separate from the one. Even your separateness is just another transformation of the one.

Teach your ego that the best way to get free is through serving the spirit while also realizing that the ego was never meant to be free, only experienced.

22

Ram Dass also said that, "The ego is a wonderful servant but a lousy master." This means that when you are identified with your ego and you think that it is all you are, you let it make the rules. When your ego starts dictating your life, you will experience suffering.

The ego lives in fear because it believes it is separate from everything else. The ego feels like it always has to prove itself to be worthy. To the ego, love is only conditional and happiness is only a pursuit. The ego makes you believe that you must be perfect to be loved by others or you must trick others into believing you're perfect. This is why you act irrationally to receive attention. When the ego is your master, you search for enlightenment from external forces. This gratification is only momentary because the ego always craves more and more.

All of these things make the ego sound evil, but the ego is not some separate force that you cannot control. It is something to be reckoned with and befriended. When you teach your ego to serve your soul, you allow yourself to find fulfillment of this physical plane while not losing yourself in the midst of the drama. Teach your ego to be aware of itself and all the emotions and ideas it brings. Watch your ego when it clings to the world like a leach and let that feeling be, while also telling your ego that it does not need to. Your ego needs to constantly be reminded that there is nothing to fear because it lives in illusion.

Spend time with yourself and get to know your ego like a best friend.

See the beauty that you see in everyone else inside yourself. Write yourself love letters, kiss your hand and lay it on your forehead, look at yourself in the mirror and see the softness in your eyes. Be gentle with yourself every second because you are your vehicle to love. You should approach a way of life where you can sit with yourself, really sit with yourself and be at peace. Every situation you face should come with ease because of the strength of the loving relationship you have with your incarnation.

You live through your body, and your life is your unique path to enlightenment. The deeper you go within yourself, the more you understand everything. Find out what fills your heart with the greatest amount of warmth and kindness and go after those things like nothing else matters.

Have a relationship with yourself where only radical honesty is welcomed. If you can admit to yourself what makes you feel bad and what makes you feel good then you can create your life around the truth of your being. So many people are scared to listen to what they really feel because they want to feel a different way. The desire to feel differently will not make you feel differently; it will only build walls between you and the truest form of yourself.

Tap into the loving consciousness that you are and listen to what your ego is saying with compassion. Through time and conscious awareness you can develop such a deep appreciation for yourself. This appreciation is one of the best things you can develop for the sake of yourself and others. When you treat yourself gently, you learn to spread that compassion to everyone else as well.

24

Taking care of yourself will always rub off on the people around you. **The best version of yourself that you can be is one that is loved by you.** To love yourself, you do not have to be impeccable; you just have to observe and appreciate your peccadilloes.

Honesty comes from facing the truth past the fear of rejection. When you are dishonest with yourself, you are actively rejecting who you are. When you reject who you are, you run farther away from cultivating a loving relationship with yourself. I know that you are scared of being judged. I know that you are scared of the things that you believe are flaws. There are parts about yourself that you wish to keep hidden. There are parts about yourself that are tender to the scrutiny of others. It is okay to have parts about yourself that you are not proud of, but hiding them will not make them go away. Repression will never bring you closer to a place of love. If you can learn to embrace your incarnation, then you can learn to flow with the way of the universe. You were built perfectly.

Your suffering is not caused by your flaws, rather your lack of willingness to accept them. And only you can accept them because everyone else is just you with their own incarnation to accept. We all have the task of accepting the body and personality that we were given. It is something that only we can do for ourselves, regardless of how others feel about us.

It is perfectly okay to be weird. It is perfectly okay to not be weird. Whoever you are, be it. Life is a lot better when you stop pretending to be something and you just be who you were made to be.

If you are so afraid of being who you are all the time, you will never allow who you truly are to flourish. You will never allow those around you to love the real you. People spend so much time rejecting their quirks, trying to fit into the mold of what they think is lovable. At the end of the day, they really only needed to be loved by themselves for being themselves.

A banana does not try to be a fig. Bananas need hot, moist, tropical weather to thrive. If it forced itself into the life of a fig where cool weather is needed to grow, the banana would suffer. The banana would never get a chance to become the sweet, neon fruit that it is. It would instead shrivel up into a dry, bitter, merely inedible piece of matter. If the banana accepted its natural chemical makeup and worked to be the best banana it could be, the banana would have the ability to thrive. You are much better off being a banana, supporting yourself with what you need, rather than trying to conform to the life of a fig.

In western society, people often think of an ego as something that comes with self-righteousness and a cocky attitude. This is somewhat true because the ego exists on pedestals. It believes that there are things below and above it. The ego craves to be seen and understood. It needs approval. It needs to be somebody. Your ego is what drives you to show off your new car or guitar skills. It wants to be known as the successful person with the new Benz or the seductive guitarist who gets all the girls. Your ego believes that there is a role to fill and it wants everyone around it to validate that role.

After I write this, I will identify as an author. My ego loves to sound pretentious, so it may want to go with "poet" instead. It's all an illusion, though. For there to be roles, there has to be separation, and we are not separate. Even though you are experiencing the role of the reader right now and I am experiencing the role of the writer, we are the same consciousness behind our roles.

It's an illusion that you are somebody. You are experiencing what it's like to be somebody, but you are beyond that somebody. On this physical plane, we operate through our bodies. That is why you feel the need to prove yourself. You feel the need to fulfill a role that will be loved and happy. Becoming one with the spirit does not mean that you have to give that up. Tuning into the wholeness of who you are will help you simultaneously be somebody while being everybody. This will bring you compassion and enlightenment. You can release the need to fill out the role of an individual. You don't have to identify with being a doctor, a banker, a wife, or a loser. You don't have to identify with being anybody at all. The illusion is that you CAN be somebody.

When this mortal life is all over, you will realize that all of it was just you. The people you were trying to prove yourself to, were just you. Do things not because they make your beliefs about who you are stronger but be because they feel right within your soul.

I am writing this book not because I want to be a famous author but because I have a book inside of me. I climb rocks not because I am a rock climber but because that is what brings me joy.

You have your unique things that make your heart explode with excitement.

Do those things not to identify with them but to live out the wishes of your heart. Buy that fancy car if it makes you appreciate being alive. Strum your guitar if the cords flow through your body like the arteries keeping your heart beating. You are nobody, but you are not nothing. You have somebody, but there is no pressure to be anybody. Do not spend your life trying to be seen; the only person who can ever see you is you.

Your incarnation has been given a certain set of parameters which your heart tells you to follow. This knowing that comes from your heart is called intuition. Your eternal spirit speaks to you through your intuition, but your ego has to be brave enough to listen. It is challenging to let go of what you've been told your entire life about making decisions. You are taught to rationalize everything and use your mind to solve problems.

So often we look past our inner knowing because society preaches the importance of evidence and logistical reasoning. Your sacred truth lies beyond your mind. It rests in a place of deep knowing, a place where you can breathe and feel aligned with your truest self. You must reprogram your mind to believe that information from your heart is the most valuable. Your heart's song is unrelenting and will not go away by you simply ignoring it. It will make you suffer with dishonesty and anxiety until you learn to trust what you know.

The direction that your heart wants to go may take immense courage to listen to. **The greatest things you will ever achieve will always involve some form of courage.** Courage does not mean that you aren't scared of the decision you have to make, but you do it while being scared. Your heart is perfectly felicitous for the trajectory of your life. The single greatest thing you can do as an individual is follow your inner knowing and let your heart sing.

The path of our hearts all lead to the same place of loving awareness. All decisions made through the heart will bring you to that place of love that you always long for. Some people spend lifetimes searching for that place where you actually feel the love that you are, but it has always just been inside of you. Sometimes this is hard to see, especially when our intuition tells us to do hard things that inflict pain and fear. Sometimes enduring this pain and fear is necessary for our growth as spiritual beings.

Never worry about the choice you have to make through your heart hurting other people. The paths of our hearts are intertwined like the roots of a tree. Your path will never hinder another being's path. All the roots rise together to build the tree of life, the tree of love. When people get wrapped up in what their egos are saying rather than their hearts, that is when they create more karma they have to face before becoming enlightened.

You are only one in 8,019,876,189 human beings. You are only one in one trillion living things. You have weird quirks and neurosis that make you such a wonderfully strange being.

No matter how small you are in the world, your presence here is the only reason why everything exists. Every single person is just as important as the next. This means that all people that exist depend on each other to be the most authentic versions of themselves so that the universe can exist in interdependent harmony.

The basis of your spiritual work comes from healing inwards so that your light can shine outwards. The universe is only perfect because you are individually you in your own unique way. It does not matter if you are a doctor, a teacher, a mother, a pizza maker or a welder. It does not matter if you make a living telling jokes, saving hungry children, or if you spend your days meditating in a cave. What you do does not make you more worthy of anything. Your worth is inherent with your existence. You are a dazzling puzzle piece to the mystery that is the universe. The incarnation you've been given is a gift that only adds to the beauty of existence. Strive for authenticity because you were made exactly the way you should be. You are always loved by the spirit, and the spirit is just you that remembers it is love.

Love the Gift

Take care of your body.

Not so that you can appear strong,

but so that you can feel strong.

So that you can show up in the world

with enough nourishment to appreciate everything life has to offer.

To run in fields, to swim in lakes,

to have unlimited patience,

all starts with a body that has been loved by its master.

Not just loved for its beauty but loved for its purpose

to serve the divinity within you.

I love the way you molded the universe into a body

Soft Moments

Sometimes I lay down with a sense

of love and gratitude swelling my bones,

a sense that I'm exactly who I should be.

Even though I've been corrupted time and time again,

there's a brief period where I feel my slate is clean,

and all I am is pure truth, pure me.

You are your best when you do what's
best for you

Unconditionally Extraordinary

You don't have to try to be a spiritual being.

You just are.

Let go of the effort you put in to be extraordinary.

Your beating heart, energy frequencies,

and emotions already tell you that you are.

There are no good or bad decisions.

There are only decisions that come from your heart or that come from anywhere else.

One will lead you closer to peace; one will take you farther away.

Humanity

I see you.

I see you as a person with complicated thoughts and emotions.

I always thought that you lived in the same world as me

but you don't.

Your whole world is so intricate and completely you.

It was easier just to write it off as the same as mine.

I've never felt this separate, but I've never been filled with so much empathy.

I looked up at a star and it told me I was beautiful.

It told me I was way bigger than I ever thought I was.

To My Ego,

Through the fire and the heat,

through the suffering and defeat,

I am here in your pocket

waiting for you to take my hand.

Through the darkness and the pain,

through the cleansing of the rain,

I am watching you grow like your motherly ghost.

You are my form.

You are my wish.

To be on earth inside of you is the greatest gift.

There is nothing to prove and no one to prove it to.

Forget the eye that wants to be seen and use it to see the oneness in everything.

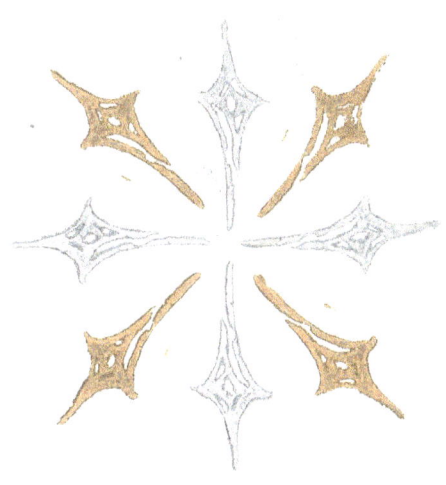

Truth

Relish this feeling.

Eat it up and remember the taste of making
decisions

directly from the core of your being,

past fear, past reason.

Feel your lungs expand with clarity

and promise to never close your ears from your
heart's voice again.

Heart Map

The decisions you've made from your heart

never took you to the wrong place.

We have been conditioned to disregard how we feel

and to rationalize our emotions,

conditioned to quiet our inner knowing.

The only place you can trust lies within.

When you listen to the wisest part of
yourself,

it will tell you,

to laugh,

to dance,

and to let go.

Lies are Carcinogenic

Ignorance is not bliss.

Pretending that destructive behavior is not harmful

does not create a peaceful mental environment.

Mendacity only builds walls between you and a life with a clear mind.

Acknowledging that the truth is the only way

will make you the person you've always felt you should be.

Radical Honesty

Give yourself the freedom to be honest with the world.

So much of your shame is confined in the wall of your heart that you refuse to share.

These barriers block you from being accepted because you won't even let them open.

Your spirit was meant to be free.

Your love was meant to be received.

The state of authenticity was meant for you to embellish,

for you to live fully.

Everyone knows what
they should do
But to actually do it,
shows who has real courage.

Love

Love is the word that is used to describe all of the good feelings in the world. It is a feeling of a warm and soft heart. Love makes you feel like you are home no matter where your body is or who you are with. It makes you feel like you could never experience hardship again because you have all the answers. That feeling of longing that you have had all your life slips away with the essence of love and you could ask for nothing more.

People have many different ideas about what love is. In our society, "love" is conditional and limited. It is acquired by being attractive, blood related, or having charismatic personality traits. Love is looked at as something that has to be earned and something that you have to prove yourself worthy to receive.

Some people find love in their relations with a family member. The earliest thing you were taught about love is that you were supposed to love your family the most. This meant that you were supposed to put them above everyone else including yourself. You were told to believe that there was some invisible bond that was holding you and your family members together, as if love were a predicament not a feeling. Most people really do love their family because they feel connected to them. It makes sense why love is easier to find in blood relations rather than spiritual relations. You can see yourself in your mothers eyes and your fathers laugh. You have siblings who you went through similar experiences with.

People associate your identity with your family and you do as well. You share a last name and unique traditions. Your family knows you at your most vulnerable state when you're a child. This familial type of love also applies to people bound through friendship or found family. Fortunate people get to experience a feeling of safety and belonging with their family, a feeling of familiarity. These sweet and maybe some bitter emotions make loving your family and friends a completely understandable concept.

Although it is easier for you to see your relation to your family, every single being is just as much you as your family is. Your capacity to love others is not limited to those with whom you share an emotional connection because you share consciousness with all beings. You are inherently connected to everything. Let your love for the people you are closest to open your heart to love all beings just as much. This mindset of abundance will help you harness an intimate relationship with anyone you meet. Your love is only strengthened through the people who make you feel safe and heard. Be that person for the stranger who is not fortunate enough to have people in their life who love them unconditionally.

Society has such a strong emphasis on romantic relationships. This societal expectation causes people to spend their entire lives looking for their other halves, as if they were never whole. We are taught that such a big part of life is spending it with a companion. The idea that we have to have someone to make us complete comes from our ego thinking we are separate.

We believe that if we have at least one person who will love us, then we won't feel as alone as we did before. The irony of this thinking is that even if you were in a room full of thousands of people, you would all be alone. Every single person in that room is just loving awareness behind the facade of being a human. Your core being is no different from anyone else's core being, there is only one.

This realization that your consciousness is always alone is called the great alone. You have always been alone, and you always will be alone. You are alone in your existence because you are everything. The paradox is that we are all alone together.

When you look at a stranger walking down the street, you are just looking at yourself. When your mother brushes your shoulder, you are just brushing yourself. When you are infatuated with that really sexy man's smile---no matter how creepy it sounds--- you just are just clinging to yourself.

Romantic relationships can spark unconditional love but they also involve a love that is through ego to ego. When people experience romance, their ego is in awe of that other ego and wants to attach itself. The traits that cause one to feel romantic love are traits of the ego and identity. Traits such as a bright smile, or pure eyes, or even a kind heart are all the traits of the human incarnation in which your consciousness is taking place. When you think of the term "significant other," this person is supposed to be someone you place above everyone else. You vow to be loyal to that one person and love them more than anyone else.

When the ego attaches itself to another ego, it comes with hardship, lust, and sacrifice. Romantic "love" causes people to attach themselves to their partner so they can not be separated from them. As we know, you are never separate from anything. This desire to obtain another being's love is all an illusion because there is no other being. We all have different nature and nurture aspects of what make us attracted to certain people, but these attractions are conditional and specific. The true loving awareness within you has no boundaries. It does not let separateness limit its ability to love. It looks at every being and sees that it is all one.

This is not to say that people cannot find love through romantic relationships. Someone's heart path might take them to a being where they feel a sense of home and belonging. They feel one with that other being and they are together in love. As Ram Dass said, "We are all just walking each other home." A partnership that brings you closer to the one, closer to the God within you is what a soulmate is. We are all meant to live the lives that we do, and many couples build beautiful lives together.

This place of bliss is not dependent on interpersonal relationships though, it is found by the realization of one. The jealousy, sadness, inferiority, anxiety, and lust that comes with romance is separate from love. These are all symptoms of attachment that stem from chemicals our brains produce such as oxytocin and serotonin.

Some people think that they have never experienced love because they feel ostracized from the world around them.

50

They feel that they are a separate being that will never be accepted for who they are. It is hard to accept love when you think it is dependent on you being lovable. All these ideas about what love is and where it is found have been tainted with human separateness. It has always been within you because it always has been you. We are love. The fact that you even exist proves that you were made out of love.

A huge part about learning to love is not only about giving it to others but learning to receive it. Sometimes we fail to open up our hearts to receiving love because we question our fortune or our worthiness. What makes us deserving of love? The beautiful thing about love is that receiving love is just as magical as giving it. Love does not have any rules, only that it is unconditionally within you. Whatever you may have done does not affect your right to love. Love is always there for you when you are willing to digest it. Accepting love can be tied to allegations of arrogance, but love is really just truth. There is nothing arrogant about accepting the truth. Allow the people in your life to be enamored with the ethereal being you are. Let people spray you with their love language, and it is up like your favorite meal. Let others' words of affirmation fill your ears with no influence from your ego questioning their validity. Look at the sun and let its light fill your chest with golden warmth. Know that your existence is one of great purpose.

When you eat the love that you are given, you excrete it out to everything around you. If someone eats a burger, they are not going to dookie out an apple.

We control the love that we receive just as we control the food we put into our mouths. Your ability to fully digest the love you are given only allows you to let it flow abundantly to everything you contact. You control how you perceive others actions, so find the love in them always. Take a smile from a stranger and squeeze the love out of it. Let the kisses from a dog tell you how sweet you are. Make all acts bestowed upon you come with the perception of love behind them. Everything that happens to you can be transformed as an act of love through the power of your perception. Then when you allow yourself to feel this love, you won't be able to help but spread it freely. We think that being humble means that we aren't allowed to accept how much we are loved, but being loved only helps us love more. When you allow yourself to be loved, you will naturally love others as well. As you are reading this, you are loved. When you stop reading this, you will still be loved. Bathe in the light from the core of your being, and you will see that your right to love is inherent with your existence.

Love is heard through the morning doves songs or the touch of a parent. It is spread through the kindness of our words and smiles of strangers. Your love is not limited to be given to one person. Love is the realization that we are only one. Everything you look around and see is just you as a manifestation of the universe. Love transcends fear, greed, lust, and anger. Love makes you look at the world and wave to it like an old friend. It can't help but make you say, "How beautiful!"

When you look through the lens of love, you will find that it is everywhere.

There is an abundance of love to give and receive. Love is not limited to the people you know or even the living. Love is looking at everything around you and saying, "I value your presence here. You make this world so beautiful." That realization that everything, everything serves a purpose within the universe will bring you love wherever you are looking.

Love is not only limited for people who do good. The spreading of love is the only thing that can awaken the knowledge of love within other people. It seems unfathomable to love someone who murders and abuses people, but what will hating them do? It will only feed into their separateness which is causing them to be despicable to other beings. You must not let others hate disrupt the love within you. The reason why people treat others so badly is because they see them as others. Love will teach anyone that they are not separate from the beings they are hurting. You do not have to tolerate vile actions, but you can choose to aim for growth through the spreading of love rather than disgust.

There is power in acknowledging the emotions that arise with your human incarnation while also keeping your heart open. On the human level war, murder, rape, and violence are so terrible. Our hearts ache at the thought of the people we care about suffering. We are built with so much empathy that we are flooded with pain when other beings suffer. We create the idea that there has to be bad people to make sense of the bad things that happen.

Condemning people into cages that feed their separateness will never teach them love. **A lack of love is the root of all the world's suffering.**

You can not control the hate other people give, but you can always control the love you give. Love is the thing we all want for the world, so you must spread it like it will save it. Love is the goal. The only way to get to the goal is by being the goal; anything else will just create more karma and confusion.

Love is infectious because it is the way. Everything else is just a front, just a phase. The goal, the only thing we ever really long for is a place where we can just be, a place where we know we are accepted and belong. That place is in love. The capacity to reach this place is always within reach, and it is always reaching out to you through the truth of your being. There is nothing else to achieve. No fancy house, supermodel girlfriend, or external validation will fulfill your soul. All of these things are just ways in which humans will think make them feel worthy. These ways to reach love are all ephemeral. Good looks fade away, assimilation takes over the happiness of being rich, and everyone who knows you as a person will cease to exist. Love is not about letting others decide how much you receive, it is about creating it through your own mind.

When you reach this place of love, it makes you want to run up to everyone you know, look them in their eyes and cry, "You are so beautiful." You want everyone to feel how important and valued they are. It makes you want to wrap the entire world in your arms and say, "Everything is alright. I am here. Love exists and it is within you!" You are just filled with such a bodily feeling of explosive compassion that you feel one with the air around you, hoping to be picked up with the wind and brought to every being. Love makes you want to live so that you can be the embodiment of its frequency. Let your actions ring with this warmth bursting out of your heart, and make your life a mission to spread this love everywhere you go.

Tell that stranger how much you love their outfit. Really look at every being you encounter and see the beauty that resides within them. Say people's name with a tongue so meaningful and sacred it that it fills them with light. Make it your goal to spread this love with every word you say. Let your feet feel a sense of home when they land on the earth. Eat your food knowing that it will sustain your body to help you spread patience and love through every endeavor. Wake with every sunrise with nothing but the intention to be kind to everything you face. Let everything you do just be another way to awaken the world to the love that it is.

In the movie, Before Sunrise, Celine says, "But isn't everything we're doing in life a way to be loved a little more?" Love is the only place we ever really want to be because it is the truth. The illusion is that you can receive love by making yourself lovable. But really, you receive love by being love. A life full of love is less about making yourself loved by other beings and more about loving other beings. When you love other beings, you are really just loving another version of yourself. You are the lover and the beloved. Who could love you other than yourself? It's all you.

Once you find this unconditional love within you, you will do anything to keep it.

It feels like a place where you have always belonged but had been estranged from for a long time. It makes you wonder why you would ever do anything but love again. This place of loving awareness is like a soft, nostalgic dream for us humans. We do all that we can to stay in that dream, but we know that inevitably we have to wake up sometime. No matter how hard we try to sleep the day away, the dream will leave our minds and we are reawakened to what we believe to be reality. It is challenging to stay in a state of loving awareness all the time. Our biology as humans and the framework of our society makes love feel like a distant dream. But really, your human incarnation is the dream and love is the reality.

If love makes me delusional,

then I never want to be sane.

A life full of love is something you create,
not a chance you leave to fate.

The High

Vulnerability is exhilarating.

The high that comes from opening your heart

and telling someone how much you care about them

is a feeling that no drug can ever beat.

Become so addicted to being in love

so that all you do is find it everywhere.

Loving unconditionally does not
make you naive.

It makes you strong.

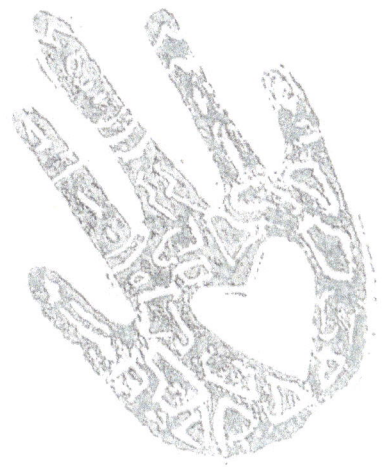

Striving

My goal is not to be perfect.

The only thing I want to be is kind.

I want to be kind to the stale faces passing by in the market,

to the squirrels that eat the fruit in my garden.

I want grace to flow through my veins like a strong river,

that can't help but burst out with every word I say.

I want everything I come in contact with to ignite a kindness of their own.

Even when my energy is depleted

or my face burns with subtle rage,

even when I do something I'm not proud of,

I want kindness to remain.

Hating yourself will not bring love to others,

and hating others will not bring love to you.

Love is the only way out.

What a beautiful way.

What to do, What to do

I am a vessel for the transfusion of love.

It does not matter if the future is blurry

or if the inevitable tasks of being a human pile up on my back.

Paper bills and ego fills could never

take away from the love I feel.

My only job is to be in the world,

even during the hours from nine to five.

There is nothing to be other than love and light.

There is nothing to fear.

There is nothing to fight.

The only thing that you can achieve in life is the love you feel while living it.

What can you love in

this

moment?

Bear the Unbearable, No Love It

It is easy to remain in a space that only blows your
hair in the right direction,

to only surround yourself with people who
remind you of your reflection,

to pick the flowers and leave the weeds,

to give love to only those who can receive.

But to challenge yourself is to grow,

and to be in a place where your grace is limited,

is where you need to go.

Unconditional

Even if the sound of your name caresses

My heart like a warm blanket or if it

stings like a frozen river,

I love love love you.

Even if the dimples in your cheeks

make me nervous of if your voice

scratches my brain the wrong way,

I love love love you.

Even if you think that your heart is only filled

with malice and you look at the world with

disgust, even if your crude jokes imprinted my

fourteen year old brain, even if you kill,

even if you steal, even if you give, even if you love,

I love love love you.

What else is there to do?

For all the times where I wasn't loving,

I'm sorry.

I forgot who I was.

Retiring the Need to be Seen

To be loved only through conditions,

the face I wear

the depth of my stare

the cities I've traveled to

and the knowledge I've acquired there

You can admire my stride only to inflate my pride

but it is just a facade that you stroke with your eyes

Showing off my person

Reaching for love in every direction

Love is different

It does not require attention

"See me, see me"

my separateness pleads

Though love does not need to see,

for there is nothing to prove.

I am already loved

and there is nothing I need to do.

To love only through conditions is just a
bite of the cake,

but to love unconditionally,

is the cake and the

whole

damn

plate.

When you have love,

you have everything

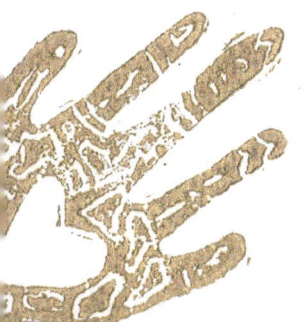

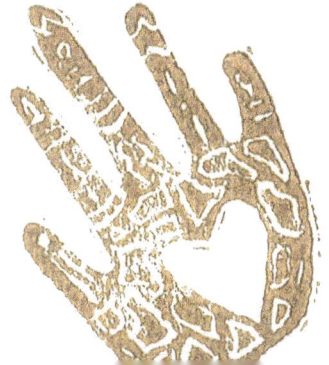

Emotions

Experiencing emotions is one of the most beautiful parts about being a human. Emotions are hard and compounding yet beautiful and ephemeral. No matter how short-lived they may be, they are as powerful as the ocean waves. Emotions are a universal human experience yet we are still so ashamed by our own sensitivity.

Most children are allowed to have big emotions and express them freely. No shame or guilt comes with the tears that stream down their faces. Children do not feel flawed when rage surges through their blood or when they are battered with confusion and fear. Even though children have less experience coping with their emotions, emotions do not get any smaller as you age. Adults are expected to always be in a state of self-regulation, but no one should ever be expected to be anything all the time. Adults are really just children who have had more time on earth. It is everyone's first time living this life with their unique body and mind. To have grace for our own emotional turmoil is to be aligned with peace and acceptance.

There is a misconception that experiencing challenging emotions means that you are doing something wrong. No one wants to feel angry, sad, or scared so people live in a way to avoid these emotions. If someone fails at the task of feeling good at the time, they feel defeated. This war against challenging emotions is a losing battle because all emotions are inevitable.

This just comes with the territory of being a human. You must stop punishing yourself for having a beating heart; therefore, you must stop punishing yourself for experiencing challenging emotions. Our biology as humans was created to experience emotions so we can navigate the world. Parts of the brain like the amygdala and hypothalamus are meant to process the emotions that come with being a human. We have hormones so that our brain can receive signals from our body. Some of these signals come through in emotion. We were created to go through the motion of experiencing emotions.

There is also a misconception that there are good and bad emotions. Some emotions are easier to handle than others, but all emotions lead you to your highest self. The greatest teachers are the emotions that you thought would never pass but always do. Allow your pain to teach you empathy. Allow your anger to teach you compassion. Allow your fear to teach you courage. All emotions work together to show you just how strong you can be, how you can turn something from debilitating and make it enlightening.

What makes living with a human mind so hard is how consuming emotions are. Without meticulous awareness of our universal consciousness, we can easily be gobbled up by these mind traps. Emotion is just energy that resides in the mind, and it can be manifested through the body. Emotions are powerful, but the consciousness within you is unaffected. Your consciousness is merely observing whatever you may be feeling.

Your consciousness watches emotions go by like clouds in the sky. This part of you knows that everything is perfect. Your consciousness notices, "Oh yeah, there's sadness", "I also see some jealousy there." It merely observes the energy but does not attach itself to the being experiencing that energy. You are not experiencing the emotions rather your ego is. To be alive is to have an ego. To be awakened is to notice that ego, and come to peace with the illusions it brings. The emotions you notice only have power if you allow them to consume who you are.

One of the most beneficial practices you can apply to your daily life is meditation. Quieting the mind allows you to connect to that part of yourself that is just pure awareness. I have made a great effort to meditate every morning and night which has allowed me to reap more benefits than ever imaginable. I learned how to meditate through the Silva Mind Control Method created by José Silva. I took a month-long meditation course on the app Mindvalley, through the teacher Vishen Lakhiani. This course changed everything about my life and the way I view any situation I'm facing. It taught me how to detach from my emotions and find the best solution to whatever problems I am facing. This month-long course taught me skills that will help me succeed for the rest of my life. I have meditated everyday for almost a year, while overcoming hardships with ease and patience. It does not matter how you meditate. You could take many classes and get many teachers to find what you like, or you could just focus on your breath and relax your mind. Life is a meditation if you allow it to be.

Your favorite hobby could be meditation for you. Your mediation practice should consist of your human heart and universal consciousness connecting as the one. There is no wrong or right way to do this. There is only your way, whatever that may be. When you take a few minutes to slow down during your busy day of being a human, you connect back to what is important and what really matters. You allow your emotions to be there without derailing your life because of them. Your meditation practice is always there for you when you need it. It is a great check point where you can remind yourself what is important to you. It is so easy to be consumed by time and the rush of daily life, but time does not exist in meditation. It is all about the present moment, which allows you to be exactly who you are with no fear. Anytime that you are observing your body sensations or your thoughts going by with no attachment, you are meditating. Any time you are fully immersed in the present moment, you are meditating. Anytime you are in love with everything that is, you are meditating.

When you realize that you are the observer of your emotions, not the emotions themselves, then you can see how truly beautiful they are. When you are experiencing fear, it is out of self-preservation. Whether you are fearful for your life, the future, or your ability to be accepted, it all stems from wanting to protect yourself. Your ego feels that it has to protect itself because it feels separate from everything. Your ego is just a scared little kid who does not know any better. Some people compare the ego to the devil or the root of all evil, but your ego does not mean to cause harm.

74

It just wants to keep you safe because it is scared of its separateness. However, there is a part of you that is never scared. This part of your consciousness does not have to fear because it is already whole and nothing can strip it away. Your consciousness IS everything. There is no hiding or secrecy. There is no shame or denying. It does not have to fear outside powers or the uncontrollable. This part of you knows that even fear is just energy in motion. Your emotions only have power over you if you attach yourself to them. Observe your fear and see how it stems from separateness. Then acknowledge that it is there and cradle it with warmth from your loving awareness. Let your ego know that it can let go of fear because only illusions can be taken away, but you last forever.

In this world, it is normal to be afraid. It is a radical to be at peace. The world feels like it is in a constant state of anxiety at all times. I bet you can think of a million things that you fear about the world. There are countless things that you want to change. The world will change; change is inevitable. But all change starts with the change that you make inside yourself. The first step to a more peaceful world that does not instill fear in every person that exists is the transformation of YOUR mind to a peaceful world. **We don't experience what is, we experience what we are.** If you feel afraid, you will see fear. If you feel tranquil, you will see peace.

Anger is a symptom of many things. It can be superficial and brought on by small irritations, or it can reside deep in your bones. You can carry it in your body with tense muscles, heavy breathing, and a fiery face.

Anger causes one a lot of mental turmoil because it does not make you feel good. We all just want to feel good or at least okay. Anger makes us feel shameful and helpless. Frustration feels like a disease you catch that completely consumes you in the present moment. Experiencing anger is bad enough, but our reactions to our anger are really the hardest things to experience. People ruin important relationships due to the anger they feel. Not only relationships with other people but the relationship with oneself gets battered with shame and distrust. We have all felt like victims to the anger we face. If only there were a way where we could just give up anger, we could be happy with ourselves. The path to a life without anger starts with you forgiving yourself when you get angry. Tune into the loving awareness that loves you unconditionally and feel its compassionate warmth. When you get angry, listen to your spirit say, "I love you anyway." You can never do anything to be unloved. Your spirit realizes that all your anger comes from you believing that what you are experiencing is real.

Ram Dass compares anger to, "getting caught in form." You are simply getting caught in your incarnation when anger takes over your mind. It is very easy to do this because you have a human body with hormones and neurons that fire surges of emotion through your mind. Your anger does not make you a bad person; it makes you a person who is getting caught in the act of being a person. Nothing is angry with you for getting angry. You are fully loved in each moment. The anger you feel only makes your life harder, and it causes you to experience hardship.

It does not change the worth of your existence.

Do not wish for a life without anger because that feels unattainable. Wishing for perfection is overwhelming and rooted in inadequacy. Wish for just this moment without anger. Take one present moment at a time with the intention to release the anger you feel. You have the power to give up anger here and now but only here and now. If you feel anger arise, do not shove it away like something that is unloved. Examine it like a part of you that needs to be tended to. Let your anger show you just the way you need to work on yourself. Welcome it with a hug and let it know that it does not need to be so serious. Your anger does not have to be a solid wall that blocks you from peace. Anger is just another cloud passing in the sky, just as white and fluffy as all the rest. It is a symptom of being human just like all the other emotions that make you whole.

Nothing can ever make you more gentle than sadness can. The emotional pain that comes with sadness carries such beauty. To feel sad about something is to show care. Your pain highlights the beauty of your human heart. It is a clear demonstration of the sensitivity within yourself. We do not desire feelings of melancholy, but they are inevitable with the empathy that resides in your body and mind. You were made to feel sad sometimes and that's okay. You are not weak. You are not failing. You are living. The emotions you feel tell you that you are alive. Your sadness is just another part of your human incarnation that makes you even more beautiful.

For those people who wake up every morning with a heavy heart that don't want to live another day, you are not your sadness.

These feelings are serving their purpose to bring you to the softest being you can be. You will not feel like this forever. Nothing lasts forever except for the loving awareness that is supporting you every step of the way. Your sadness is a wound that needs your love. It does not need to be rushed or shamed. You will heal. Your healing journey starts with you loving yourself with every ounce of emotion that you have. Feeling depressed is something that no one would ever wish upon anybody. It can feel as if every ounce of happiness has been erased from your body. It feels scary and lonely. You are not alone in your darkness, for every being has felt the depth of a desolate place without love. Take the sadness that you feel and turn it into empathy for others. Every single person that has ever existed has felt gut-wrenching pain. Every person has experienced feelings of complete darkness with no hope. We are all deserving of compassion. We all deserve each other's empathy. Let your pain remind you how hard it can be to exist sometimes. Treat every person that you see as if they could be going through the hardest day of their lives because they could be. Make it your mission to give everyone the compassion and love that you always craved. Let every soul you touch feel the shred of light that you desperately needed in your darkest times.

When you are feeling low and nothing seems worth all the pain, try to give others light while not restricting any for yourself as well. Let your pain remind you how important love is. Sadness is not limited to those who have an intimate relationship with death or loss. It does not only weigh on those with no friends or money. Sorrow is felt by those who are rich, those who have everything they could ever ask for. People in big houses, little houses, multiple cars, or none at all, feel pain and darkness. Sadness creeps in broken homes with abuse or in suburban houses with two stable parents.

78

The life of the party, the ridiculously beautiful woman, the man who dances while walking down the street all experience sadness. It will catch you from time to time no matter where you are in the universe. Everyone experiences pain. The way that you turn your pain into something powerful is what makes you strong.

Emotions are a part of the game of being alive. Life is like a beautifully dramatic movie. Some parts of the movie are gut-wrenching to witness. When your favorite character dies or when your favorite couple is torn apart by society, you are flooded with despair. These movies only have the beauty they do because of the emotion they invoke within you. If a movie caused you to feel nothing, not even laughter or joy, it would have no value to you. The movies that we love so dearly are the ones that make us feel alive, and they only make us feel alive because of the emotions they cause us to feel. Our egos are like the characters and our spirit is like the actors. Your spirit knows that life is just a dream, just as the actors know they are just in a movie, but the characters are the ones who experience the emotion.

Life is filled with beauty, and that beauty only comes with emotion. Honor the emotions that arise with your human heart, and love them like the potent lessons that they are. This mortal life is nothing without the sensitivity of our hearts. All that exists is what fits together to make the universe so grand. You are whole with all your gentle, human beauty.

No Use to Sit and Wonder Why

I don't know why I'm here,

but I don't think it matters anyhow.

There are millions of synchronicities that

lead to this very moment.

So many kisses and hugs,

infinite creations and transformations.

But I am here in this body,

with this heart that only lasts a lifetime.

So I am going to love,

and I am going to relish the tears

of the ephemeral, sensitive heart.

All Encompassing

Can you see the beauty of it all?

Not just in the quiet moments with

soft eyes and dreamy thoughts

or white lilies and green moss.

Can you feel the purpose of your agonizing pain

and can you love that darkness just the same?

The depth in your heart never changes

even when your thoughts are tainted with messy rage.

Your life has only one hue because everything is just you.

You who can fly through emotions like a meteor through space,

infinite possibilities, though never displaced.

Beauty is not found in a world that is only bliss.

Wholeness is what creates the beauty that is inherently within.

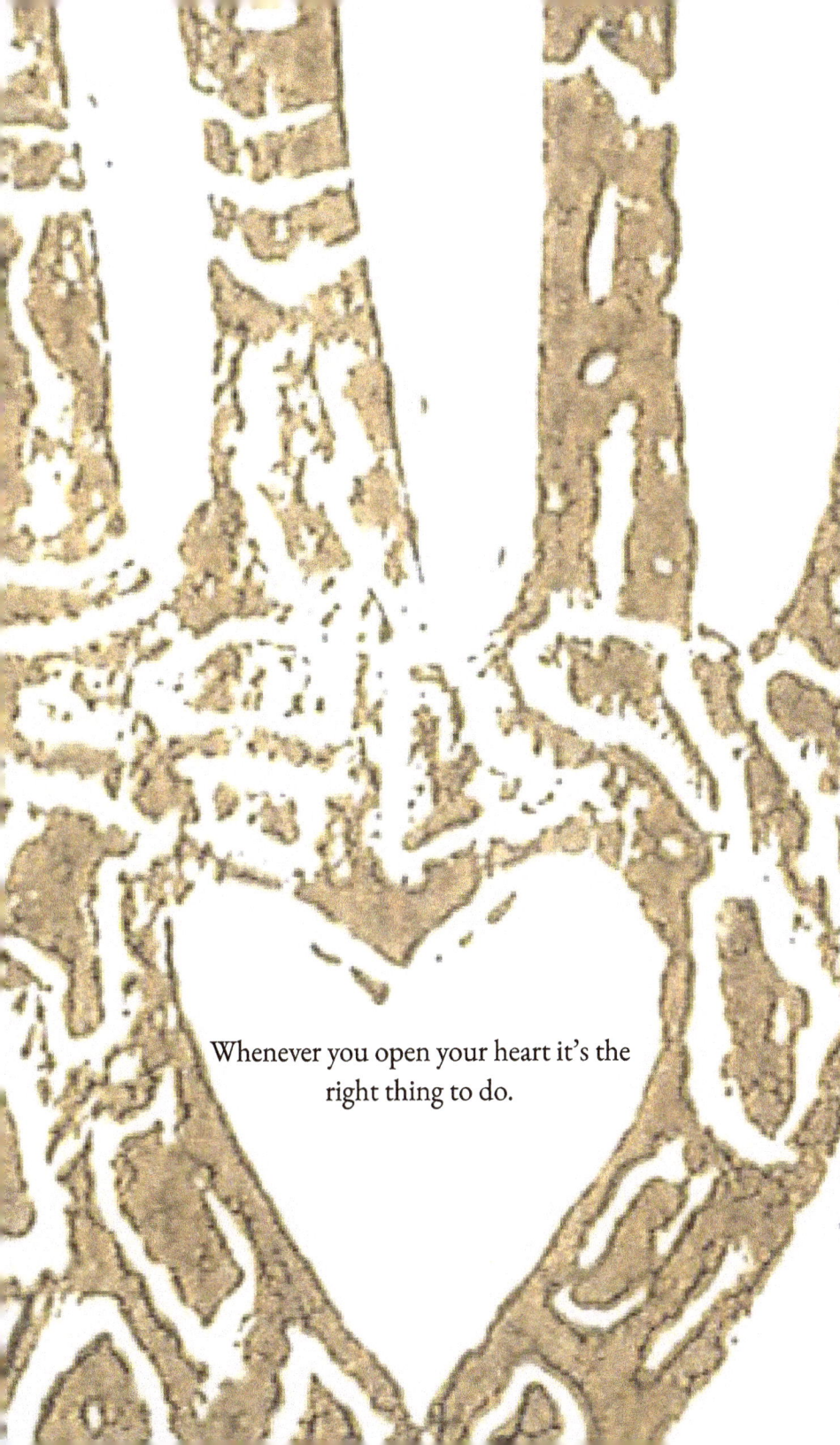

Whenever you open your heart it's the
right thing to do.

Allow

You can't be in human form and

expect yourself not to feel human things.

It's okay to desire.

It's okay to feel emotions.

It's okay to enjoy.

It's okay to indulge.

The human part of us is what keeps us alive.

If you have to remind yourself that life is precious

every hour,

every minute,

every second,

DO IT.

Because, it is.

Do not feel bad if it takes effort to notice all of life's beauty.

Effort is required for almost all great things.

Every moment of distress is an
opportunity to make peace.

A letter to my darkness,

You engulfed me with despair. You pushed my head underwater and left me gasping for air.

Life was heavy and unbearable with you, yet this is me on the other side, completely through.

You left a pit in my stomach, but now it has blossomed.

I am wiser and stronger. I hold no bitterness against you any longer.

I am free from your cage with a gentleness that floods the world with light.

You taught me how to love. You taught me how to fight.

I owe everything to the glimmers of hope that lead me through the pain.

They all brought me here to a place where I can see the personal gain.

You were my teacher wrapped in disguise.

To experience you fully was the ultimate prize.

I won compassion and courage, beauty and sorrow.

I gained a strength that I will always let people borrow.

I welcome you now with open arms, the yin and the yang.

You keep the world growing, with the joy and the pain.

Thank you for the ride to this place of love.

Next time I will greet you without fear, just a big, warm hug.

Doesn't it feel good to be gentle with yourself?

Carrots

But there is no such thing as total darkness.

And the truth is, love is in every molecule you will ever interact with.

Don't worry about losing joy or the goodness in life.

It is something that cannot be lost, only temporarily dimmed.

Eat more carrots, light a candle, be a flame:

Find a way to see better in the dark.

I Will Not Be Perfect

My heart is telling me that I will be making mistakes for the entirety of my life.

I will get angry and I will lose my temper.

I will say things that I am not proud of.

I will be far from perfect.

My heart is also telling me that my suffering is not because of my flaws,

rather my resistance to accept them.

I will live with my vices and I will be loved anyway.

We are Fed Fear

To live in peace,

is to rebel against the illusion that anything is ever wrong.

Fear lives in your water.

It is injected into you like a vaccination preventing indifference.

Rise above the doom that floods society.

Your tranquility is not radical;

it's inherent.

Throwing Away The Key is The Key

There is no key to everlasting happiness.

You cannot unlock the door to a room with only bliss.

There is no door nor room.

There is only what you experience and what you let get consumed.

Peace is not a constant state.

It is an underlying awareness of the beauty in the struggle.

It is the ability to let go of what comes when it inevitably does.

Life is a continual lesson on learning how to juggle.

Don't wait for your life to turn into something easy.

You will be waiting forever.

It will be hard, yet the most beautiful thing you will ever endeavor.

To be soft is to be free,

free from the fear of being human.

Presence

The one thing that we can count on as humans is that everything is always changing. Our bodies are aging, our emotions are shifting, and the world around us looks different everyday. Nothing will be the same in a year or even in an hour.

The only moment where change is irrelevant is the one right now. It simply does not matter what has been or what will be. This point in time is where all the power you have is. You only have the power to really be here because you can never truly be anywhere else. You have always just been in this moment.

From before the time you were born, all the way past your death, the time will always be now. Whenever you ask yourself, "What time is it?" the answer will always be the same, "The time is now." The illusion of time makes us think that there are separate moments defining our lives. Time is what people define relative to the start and the end. Your human incarnation had a start when you were born and it will have an end when you die, but you are beyond time. You have always just existed and you always will. There is no start or end to your consciousness. It is always just living in the here and now. There is no other place to be.

Since we are in a human incarnation, we are constantly experiencing change. With change comes uncertainty, and with uncertainty comes fear. It is so easy to fear the future or fear the inevitable changes that are bound to happen.

We spend so much time thinking about what will be even though there is no predicting nor controlling the outcome of anything. It is useless to devote the present moment to planning out the future when no actions that you take will affect what is bound to happen. There is no part of you that needs to have it all figured out. It is simply impossible to plan life to workout exactly the way you want it to go. Life has a funny way of not always giving us what we want but giving us what we need.

No matter what your future holds, you will never be in the wrong place. You may experience feelings of doubt, but even those feelings of doubt serve a purpose. Everything you go through, you are meant to. The wrong place does not exist because you are everywhere. People think that home is where you come from, but home is actually just a part of you. Wherever you are, home is, and you are everywhere, in everything. Home is a tree, your body, a friend, even a jail cell. **There are no wrong paths; there is only the path.** Worrying about the path is just a product of you thinking that you are separate from the path.

Not only does the future distract us from the here and now, but the past has cunning ways of sneaking into the present moment. As a person, our pasts are important. They teach us who we are and who we want to be in the future. Our pasts are filled with laughter and reminiscences of hope. They are also filled with sorrow and haunting memories. The worst thing that you can do for yourself is believe that your past was wrong in any way. The resistance to accept what brought you to this moment will affect your ability to tap into the loving consciousness that you are.

94

When we look back at the past, we often romanticize our memories. Sometimes moments seem so much sweeter when you're looking back on them compared to when you experienced them in the moment. Even hardships that you went through have a certain nostalgia to them that make the challenging emotions you faced softer and easier to swallow. This is because of the realization that you made it out okay. You realized that you survived. It is hard to see how situations will work out when you are experiencing them, but they always do. There is a part of you that will always be okay.

So much of our joy gets robbed from the present moment by anxiety that things will never pass. But then, they always do. If you can tap into the part of yourself that knows that it will always be okay, then you can relieve yourself from the agony of impatience. Whatever you are going through, it will be okay, so you might as well be okay now. Give up the worry and the fear. You know that the outcome is peace. No matter how long it takes to get there, it will always be waiting for you in the present moment. Luckily, it is always the present moment.

To be fully present is to realize that you have always just existed. You were never created because you always just were. The past is defined as the moment before this one. The future is defined as the moment after this one. Your ability to appreciate the past and the future brings the peace that is always within your conscious being. This peaceful acceptance is always available to you. It is the only thing that always exists and never changes.

Being fully immersed in the present moment is truly a high for us humans. We all have our ways of getting high (being present): Drugs, art, movement, eating, sex, skydiving, ect. What causes you to forget your entire life in a single moment? What makes you stop thinking about anything else other than what is right in front of you? This is your vehicle to the present moment. Presence is so addicting because it is ecstasy. When you are completely entrapped by the present moment, you forget to eat and sleep. You forget that you are even a person with a life. You become one with whatever your hands touch. Your mind gets a rest from its constant juggling of thoughts.

When people deal with addictions, their way of getting present is harmful. Some people are most definitely more chemically inclined to certain ways of getting high. Although not all ways of getting high are as sustainable as one another, they all lead to the same place, being the present moment.

When you are present, you are actively embodying God. This feeling feels so fleeting to us because our ego's end up chiming in reminding us we have bills to pay, jobs to attend, books to read, food to make, and people to take care of. There are so many tasks that pile up on our backs; the list is never ending. There will always be more things to learn, bigger things to achieve, more stuff to own, more places to see, better traits to have. At a superficial view, the present moment can seem just so... un-whole. Our ego's tell us that it is never enough. And if you do completely identify with your ego, then it never will be enough. Your ego can never have it all because that is the nature of a human incarnation.

Your spirit knows that it does not need to have anything because it is everything. When you are aligned with the universe, God, spirit, there is no place to be other than present. If there is nothing to achieve, no one to be, nothing to have, nothing to see, then there is no reason to be anywhere other than right where you are.

People often overlook the joy being present brings. We are susceptible to the illusion that the vehicles that bring us to presence (what makes us high) is what causes our joy. What actually causes the joy is being present.

You can test this out for yourself right now by closing your eyes and letting your awareness transfer right to the feeling of air pouring in and out of your nostrils. Notice the sounds around you that are forcing your mind to gravitate to the present moment. Take three breaths fully immersed in the moment while letting your mind notice the air coming in and out of your nose. Could you feel yourself supported by the present moment? Did you notice that there is peace in the here and now? This state of awareness is available to you at all times. It can be easier to reach during some times than others, but it is always here nonetheless.

We all want to feel peace and be loved. We are all chasing the present moment whether we know it or not. You do not need to run to catch the moment, it is right here for you when you are ready to stop chasing and to start being.

You do not need drugs to get high. You need to stop wanting and start appreciating. There is nothing that this moment can't offer you. It is all here. Your ability to be here is your ultimate ticket to unconditional joy.

Only few things are certain in this world,
one being that this moment will pass.

Be here now so you can be in the next
one when it comes.

What Is

Do not let the rumination of what could have been better

steal your gratitude and joy.

It could have been different in an infinite number of ways,

but none of them would have been right.

What is right, is what is.

No amount of overthinking will change the past.

No amount of planning will make the future perfect.

All there is to do is appreciate what you've gone through,

and love yourself while growing every step of the way.

No moment is ever more special than another.

Preciousness is found wherever your feet are laying

and your eyes are looking.

As long as your heart is fully where you are,

you are seizing that gift of which is the present.

Existentialism

The most fulfilled people I know

do not have unlimited free time or money.

They aren't painted with conventional beauty,

and they don't possess any divine talents.

They still have to fold their laundry and vacuum their carpets.

The only difference between these people and everyone else is

that they know the beauty that lives within the mundane.

They know that each moment is only as special as you make it.

These people make each moment purposeful to the

trajectory of their life.

They know that it matters not what they do but how they feel
about what they are doing.

Living through your loving awareness means giving up excessive rumination

and seizing your ability to find love right where you are.

Take each present moment at a time.

Your life will move forward, but your love will always remain.

Find it here.

Find it now.

One Day at a Time

Maybe today I can let go of all the things

that I've done in the past.

Maybe today I can release myself from shame

and write a new narrative.

And when tomorrow becomes today,

I will do the same.

Success is only measured by your ability
to find joy in this moment.

Forever With Me

There is no past version of you.

There is no future version of you.

There is only you.

You travel through this lifetime without ever leaving yourself.

Everything you have experienced, you've been there.

Everything you will experience, you will be there.

Your hands are the same ones that cusped the blanket wrapped around your bare, freshly born body.

Your same eyes that met the earth with wonder,

fill your soul with light each waking morning.

Here you are with that same internal voice that guided you through kindergarten and read picture books without looking at the words.

The same voice that supported you through years of experimentation and new experiences,

that comforted you through debilitating fear and paliple joy.

You are never gone.

You are your person.

Celebration

We rarely look back and realize what we once longed for is now in the palm of our hands.

This isn't because we didn't receive our wishes.

It must be that we've forgotten the yearning

or we are so distracted by our new desires.

You must notice your victories and hold them close to your heart.

Don't let them flee with assimilation and more longing.

You've come a long way;

cherish it, right at this moment.

The Drive Home

Even though looking out at the bare, snowy planes lacks a feeling of growth and change,

there is a subtle wrinkle in your personality.

Not one of distress but one of squinty eyed laughter.

The effects of walking on new parts of the world never truly flee,

for you are found through diversity.

Time has a way of stealing your emotions,

but the quick smell of a rose can make you dream of a garden.

And a cold breeze hitting your lungs will take you back to that snowy peak.

Your adventures are never forgotten;

they are molded into the very person you are in the present.

You are decorated with your memories,

seasoned by the past.

You are a cast iron skillet,

whose flavor will always last.

Shame

I know you want this time to pass and this day to be over.

You want a clean slate and an empty conscience.

Slow down.

Breathe.

Wanting the hours to go by faster will not speed up time.

Being mad at yourself for your problems will not make them go away.

Your future starts here with the gentle decisions you make now.

Later

All the things I want to do run through my hands like water.

I want to do it all.

I want every experience to enrich my soul with all the passion life can squeeze.

But I wait

I wait

I wait

For when?

For later.

The later that never comes.

The later that leaves once it is spoken.

Putting my dreams into the hands of the future.

Putting my heart into my dreams and watching them float away with what will never arrive.

God Lives In My Nostrils

In the present moment lies your eternal love.

You will not find it if you look backward.

You will not find it if you look forward.

You must breathe it in from the air right beneath your nose.

This is where you can find yourself.

Everywhere is here.

Everything is now.

Judgment

The minute you judge something, the minute you disconnect from the universe. Everything that exists is just a transformation of you. When you judge something, you are not only limiting its potential, but you are simultaneously getting trapped in your own ego. The place where judgment comes from is the belief that you are separate from what you are ridiculing, which is the ego thinking. When you are aligned with your truest self, you are aligned with everything. You have no right to judge anything because it is all you. When you are in a place of love, you do not have the capacity to judge anything because you see that it is all one.

Thoughts that arise like, "He's bad or she's good" put unnecessary cages on people. The idea of good and bad comes from our human brains trying to categorize things. Polarizing words like, good, bad, right, and wrong are all subjective. Our own inner worlds create what fits into these categories. There is really only one category: What is. There are no mistakes. The things that happen may cause hardship, but it is not bad, it is just hard. Every circumstance serves its own purpose, and every being is exactly the way they should be.

Just because someone or something is different does not give you a right to judge it. Different is a relative term. There are always going to be people different from you. You are always going to be different from other people.

You live in a world that only you know. Everyone else has just as complicated of a life as you do. Your way of living is not the right way. There is no "right way." What you do is what you do because of the things you are taught, the people you are surrounded by, and your own unique perceptions of the world. The things other people do is because of what they are taught and their own thoughts revolving around the world. Giving up self-righteousness is going to help you seek truth and let go of the burden of being right and wrong.

Life is really hard when you judge everything around you. Judgment causes anger and jealousy. It causes your body to be inflamed with wasted energy. Tainting your precious thoughts and words with crude commentary only brings you down. There is no use in having any sort of malice towards another being because their purpose is to be exactly who they are. You do not have to agree with everything someone does or says. It is okay to not want to partake in behavior you find repulsive, but refraining from judging will only help you go after the things that are aligned with yourself. Focus not on the things that bring you hate but the things that bring you love. Your energy goes wherever your mind goes. Let your energy not be attacking what you don't want but supporting what you do want.

Someone's actions might make you feel angry or annoyed, but these emotions are simply because of your perspective. If someone says something hateful and you get hurt by it, it is only because of the way you see that other person.

If you see them as a separate being who has a problem with you, then that perspective is going to cause feelings of inferiority within you. The truth is, how we treat other people is really just a reflection of how we feel about ourselves. If you see the person who said that hateful comment through the lens of their problem, you no longer give that person power to affect how you feel. **With the realization that all of our own judgments are just reflections of our own inner worlds, we release the power others judgments have over us.**

This also means that you must acknowledge that any judgment you feel towards anyone else is just because of your own perspective. Take responsibility for any judgments that arise in your mind and observe them like the nails on your fingers. Judgments will always come to our minds, for we are human. You are naturally inclined to feel disgust towards things that go against what you identify with. Even the most loving people experience judgmental thoughts, but they do not attach themselves to their thoughts. They see that the thought came from their own ego, just like the nails on our fingers are a part of our body. They then let the thought go without identifying with it, just like we are not the nails on our fingers. We have judgmental thoughts because we are human. We should not judge ourselves for having malicious thoughts because that only sends out more judgmental energy. Observe the thoughts that arise with your ego and teach the ego that it is not separate from whatever it's judging.

If you look at someone and despise their mustache, it is your responsibility to understand where your judgment comes from.

Maybe you met someone who caused you pain and they had a mustache. Maybe you are insecure about your own mustache or not having a mustache, or maybe it is just not your specific taste in facial hair. All of these reasons do not make the mustache ugly, it just makes it ugly to you. **Just as beauty is in the eye of the beholder, judgment is as well.** Get to know your judgments intimately so that you can understand what part of you they are coming from. When you understand the reason behind the way you feel, you have an easier ability to let them go.

When you think that someone else is judging you, you are really just judging yourself. You have an insecurity that is tender to the scrutiny of others. If you had brown hair and someone called you a "dumb blonde," you would not take offense to that comment because you know it is not coming from a valid place. But when someone insults and insecurity of yours, you validate it with the judgment you already feel towards yourself. All judgments from other people are invalid because they are just a reflection of their inner worlds. Those who are completely enlightened do not judge anything because they have the realization that everything is just the way it should be. They also are not affected by others' judgments because they know that they are only thoughts coming from the ego. When others' judgments affect something within you, you know that they hit a sensitive area within you. This tenderness is not something that they can heal by apologizing. Only you can heal this part within yourself because, under everything, it is just the judgment that you have against yourself.

When something ruffles your feathers, it is a blessing because it shows you what you need to heal within yourself. If someone's actions offend you, take the opportunity to dig deep within yourself and find out why. We are responsible for the way we feel. The only way to heal is to dig past the surface level and find out what is really hiding deep inside yourself.

Every single person in the world deserves your unconditional compassion. When you feel the need to judge another being, picture them as a little kid. See them with complete innocence and fear. Whatever is causing you to judge that person, has not always been a part of them. They developed it through their environment. Every person is just doing their best with what they know. If people knew how to love, they would because it feels so good. When people are unkind, it is only because they don't know how to be anything else. It is a shame to watch people struggle to be the loving beings they are, but it makes it all worse when you limit them as "bad people." Give them a chance to find the love that is within them. Teach them how to love by loving them.

Gossiping is a recreational activity for mass amounts of people. It can be so addicting to talk badly about other people. Once you start, it is hard to stop because something in us feels better when we put other people down. This feeling does not last long because pointing out other people's flaws does not make ours any smaller; it only gives us a new flaw. Engaging in judgmental conversations only makes you a judgmental person.

There is nothing good that can come out of shaming others just for the fun of it. When you are in a situation where gossip is happening around you, find the softness within yourself. Go to that place where you are all one, and see the being that you are judging as a different form of you. Try to enlighten people around you who are caught in the gossip. Always stick up for the victim of bitter commentary because they are unconditionally deserving of compassion. If you were being talked badly about, you would want someone to stick up for you. You know that you are just a person who has had moments that you are not proud of. You would never want these moments to define you, so don't let these low moments define someone else.

Most people would not be blatantly rude to a person if they were standing right next to them, so why do people say mean things about people when they are not there? Every single person is inside of you at all times. There is no hiding from anyone because your consciousness hears everything. When your consciousness hears your words of judgment, you are automatically bringing your frequency down from a place of love to a place of separateness. You can not hide from your darkness, but you can do your best to release it. You do not have to spread negativity to fit in. Engaging in negative talk for the sake of wanting to be accepted will only give you a sense of acceptance from people who don't know how to accept. If they did, they would not spend their time judging. The only place you need to be connected to is within, and you do this by sticking to what feels good in your heart.

We are all just trying to do our best with the challenges that arise on this physical plane. Living on earth is hard. Having a body is hard. That last thing we need in this world is more hate. People do not need to be judged to be changed. **They need to be loved.** You do not need to judge to feel better. **You need to love.** Releasing judgment seems like a massive task at first, but all you have to do is surrender to the truth. Acceptance in nature. There is a part of you that is never judging, yet always observing. Rely on your consciousness to guide you through the world with curiosity not hatred.

How beautiful it is to look into
the eyes of another

and see nothing short than a
divine creation of the universe.

How could I possibly hate what
the stars have created,

for we were all made from the
same dust.

Sonder

The key to understanding other people

is not about agreeing with them.

It is about swapping your eyes out with theirs,

transferring your awareness into their unique body,

looking down at their hands as if they were your own.

You must realize that their life is just as real to them

as yours is to you.

Projection

Do not let others' thoughts about you limit who you are.

Thoughts hold truth like a strainer full of water.

What each person thinks is their own karmic predicament.

Leave the cage.

You are limitless and free.

I release the judgment that I don't deserve to be happy.

Responsibility

To not take anything personally

means to take responsibility for the cause of your judgments.

Judgment is not something that is bestowed upon us.

It comes from inside.

It is created by our inner worlds

and always has something to do with our own insecurities.

Acknowledge that all feelings of judgment belong to the beholder.

There is power in knowing your judgments are personal

because there is bliss in knowing that others' judgments are as well.

Your judgmental thoughts towards yourself are limiting your capacity to be kind.

You are just as deserving of compassion as everyone else around you.

Growth starts with the movement of energy.

The energy you want to give starts with yourself.

Interdependence

Being dependent on others is looked down upon in society, yet we are all dependent on each other. You came into this world through another person, and you will leave this world imprinted by thousands of different people. When you are a baby, you need people to raise you into an independent person. Though you learn how to walk on two feet and wipe your own ass, you are still dependent on others throughout your entire life. The food you eat, clothes you wear, the house you live in was created by other beings. Your life has been painted with every person you've ever met. You are who you are because of who everyone else is.

We are not not only dependent on each other; we are dependent on nature and our eco systems. We have to count on nature to sustain our health through food and water. We depend on all the animals to keep the environment healthy. There is a chain of dependency that flows throughout the universe. Even nature depends on nature. The flowers need the rain and the sun; the bees need the flowers. The tree produces oxygen that we all depend on, but the trees first need to be supported with water and soil. Nature is only as beautiful as it is because of the way it works together as a system. Every single organism is crucial to the state of the environment. This is the same case for humans. We are all one system that works better together. There is no burden in supporting each other because we are all one.

Do you think that the clouds get annoyed for having to water the flowers? Of course they don't because there is no separateness in nature. When one organism supports another, it is just supporting a different form of itself. When you support another being, you are supporting yourself. **The stronger our interdependence is, the more beautiful we are as a whole.**

Independence makes us feel safe and powerful. If we do not give others the right to affect us, then we can control our own happiness. This is very true to a point, but blocking others out of your life will not bring you peace. Whenever you are rejecting anything, your ego is making itself separate from the world. The ego believes that it can be independent, but there is a whole network of energy behind physical form running the universe. We are all connected, no matter how hard you try to run or hide. You can isolate yourself in the woods and never see another soul with your eyes again, but you will always be connected to every living thing through energy.

The desire to not be dependent on others comes from us feeling separate from them. We want to create safe little bubbles so we do not get hurt by things we cannot control. Even though you cannot control how other people act, you can control how you perceive their actions. It is up to you to remain unattached to the way people act while being connected to the spirit behind their actions. You do not have to worry about not being accepted by other people. You are perfectly lovable the way you are and others' capability to accept you has nothing to do with you. At the root of our being is love.

The person that has trouble accepting who you are is still working through their spiritual journey. All you can control is the love you give and your openness to receive love from others.

Independence is a way for the ego to grow and comfort itself. Without the ego, there is no independence. There is only one consciousness behind everything. This consciousness makes all forms dependent on each other, concluding to the harmony of the universe. Someone across the world from you is doing something right now, impacting which way the universe turns. While they are not directly impacting your life, they are affecting the direction of the universe. Newton said that, "Every action has an equal and opposite reaction." These reactions spread across the world like ripples in a lake. We all depend on each other for the life we experience, but our attitude towards our own lives is what we can control as independent beings.

Some people think that by isolating themselves they can reach an intimate relationship with their highest self. Some periods of isolation may help your mind connect with the universe, but you can never really be disconnected from the universe. Your spirit is there in every person you meet. There comes a point when you realize that being with others does not weaken your relationship with yourself. You need to see past the illusion that others are separate from you to connect with every version of yourself. You are not betraying yourself by enjoying the company of others; you are only valuing your incarnation. A good balance between alone time to center yourself and social time to connect with other parts of yourself is a good way to honor your biological needs.

Humans are social creatures. Our biology supports our need for love and belonging. Fighting against biology will make your life much tougher than if you learn to work with it. Part of being a human is socializing with other humans. Our egos make this quite a challenge. Whether you have problems with accepting other people or not being accepted by other people, these feelings arise from us living in separate human bodies. We do not have the power to ever fully understand what is going on in others minds which frankly, scares us immensely. It is frightening to look into the eyes of another and have no idea what they are thinking about. We fear that they are thinking about how annoying we are and how much they don't like us. We fear that we will be ostracized from the people around us because of who we are. If someone were to be judging you, it is only a reflection of their ego. The consciousness between you and them is only loving awareness. At the core of your being, you are always loving and are always loved. When you look at people through this view, you will have no problem letting go of whatever they may be thinking because it has nothing to do with you.

Having friends and people you care about is a good thing when there is true loving awareness that is connecting you to them. When you have a relationship that is harnessed through love, there is no insecurity or questioning of your worth. If your friend decides to spend some time away from you, you let them go because that is what they need to do. They really can't go anywhere because they are already within you. They can take their body all the way across the world, but they can never really leave your side because they are just you. Let people flow in and out of your life like the seasons taking their course. Being interdependent does not mean that you have to attach yourself to the people you care about. Real unconditional love comes without attachment.

Some people become too codependent on other people and they lose themselves in the relationship. This stems from problems of attachment. When you give another person the ability to dictate the way you feel, you are too connected to your ego. When you are connected to your spirit, you are unattached to the forms of the universe while simultaneously being connected to everything. Your consciousness is not dependent on anything else because it never changes. There is always pure loving awareness within you that you can tap into at any moment. When you are feeling anxiously codependent, your consciousness is watching knowing that it is just an ego trip. Whoever enters or leaves your life does not change your spirit.

You can harness a loving relationship with whomever you please because it is just created by you loving them. You just have to see the beauty within them and treat them like the divine incarnations they are. Loving relationships are not about wanting to be loved. The desire to be loved comes from your ego wanting to be coddled. Your spirit already knows that it is loved. **When you love another being, your spirits are just meeting in a place of love.** There is no giving or receiving of love between spirits.

128

All of your relationships with other beings can come from this place. When you see others through this light, you cannot get hurt by their coming and going. This view makes interdependence a sustainable truth, not an insecure attachment. When you find yourself feeling insecure with a group of people, stop focusing on what they are thinking about you. Focus on how beautiful they are and how much you love them. Your actions will then be filled with authenticity and kindness. You will be less worried about saying the right thing because your objective is no longer to make yourself look good. When you live in the role of the lover, it does not matter who is loving you because you are doing your part of being love.

When you reach a spiritual enlightenment and you learn about the power of your consciousness, it might make you want to spread these teachings to the people around you. Though, not everyone is ready to digest the truth of their being. We all want each other to find happiness. It makes sense that you want to teach the people around you about a perspective that helps you enjoy life more. You just want them to find peace and love. Even though your intentions might be good, forcing any point of view onto anyone never works out. Each person will find their way to peace when they are ready. When you hear people being hateful or spreading negativity, it can be very easy to become infuriated with those people. You start asking yourself, why don't they understand? Why is everyone so trapped in what doesn't matter? These thoughts take you out of your spirit and bring you back to separateness. Now there is "them" and there is "you."

The best way to help others find this loving way of existing is through being the message that you want to teach. You never have to tell anyone how to behave. You only have to behave in the way you want others to be. When you live your life spreading kindness and love, you are actively teaching others to do the same. Change starts with you being what you want the world to be more of. You can not expect anyone else to be anything. Only you can control your actions. When you expect things from other people, you are not letting the universe do its work. Everyone is exactly who they should be. Don't count on anyone to be anything because they just need to be who they are. Let people be who they are while remaining true to who you are. I know that the spiritual journey can feel lonely at times. You are being divinely supported by everyone at all times, even if you can't see it. **Everyone exists to make sure that you experience life exactly the way you need to.**

The formula for connection is a mixture of appreciation and honesty. You must focus on appreciating how the other person is just a different manifestation of you. When you are speaking to anyone, you are speaking directly to God. Humans are just God with a costume on and many layers of separateness. Find the beauty in every person you speak to. Let love swell your bones when you look into the eyes of another. Let your consciousness say, "I see you in there. It's just me. It's just me."

The second part is honesty. You must open yourself up and let yourself be seen. When we hide, we do it because of fear of rejection or fear that we are wrong.

When you speak to someone while holding back your truth, you never allow that other person to connect with who you are. If they cannot accept your truth then they still have some spiritual work to do. All you can do is open your heart and let yourself be naked in the face of others. Hiding only causes you to feel repressed shame in the relationship you have with yourself. You may think that hiding who you really are will save you from losing important relationships, but only real relationships are built with honesty.

The combination of appreciation and honesty creates vulnerability. When you are vulnerable with others, you allow there to be intimacy. We all crave intimacy. We want others to see who we are while knowing exactly who they are. This can only happen when you open your heart to love and to be seen, pushing past fear. Let go of the fear that comes with intimacy because it is all you. Every person you meet is a creation of your consciousness. The connection between you and others does not have to be built; it just has to be found.

The best impression you can leave on
someone is not admiration of your
goodness, rather the inspiration to be a
good one's self.

Let People Be

Life is not about convincing people to see the world the same way you do.

It's about making them feel safe in their own world.

Save people by loving them while they find their way.

Your path is right for you and theirs is right for them.

Let the universe unfold as it should.

People will bloom when they are ready.

Rest in your love.

Rest in your truth.

The moths do not need to be chased with the flame.

They will all come flying to your light in divine time.

There is nothing to fear when showing a
stranger your heart.

We are all

friends

lovers

one.

The Light Will Prevail

You control how other people behave

like you control the sun fading away.

People will always be caught in fear,

lost in greed, power, and lust.

The night will always come.

Only you can control how you cope with the day turning into
dusk.

You are a star that keeps the world from utter darkness.

Without you, black holes would consume.

The world needs your light like the night needs the moon.

A lonely star is the bravest of them all,

to keep shining in a desolate place.

Bathe in your courage.

Carry with you your grace.

You keep the world from sinking into the ephemeral night.

Day will always come,

guided by your light.

I am the winner, the loser, and everything in between.

You're not helping anyone else out by being dishonest.

The path of your truth can do no harm.

The thing we all need yet don't know we want:

honesty

honesty

honesty

Masterpiece

Each person is a work of art that is dependent on
all the works that came before them:

The music

The poetry

Birds singing

A kiss

A glance

Nuanced decisions

Strands of courage

Leaps and heaps of failure

A mosaic that you are,

created from the beauty of the universe

Carbon and inspiration we are built upon

```
Slip, fall, forget, cry,
puke, laugh
```

Having a body is embarassing.

Being a person is embarrassing.

No one is immune.

And if you think they are,

you are simply mistaken.

So let go of your blunders.

People only remeber their own anyway.

Perspective

Life is a dream. Everything feels real when you are experiencing it; but when you wake up, you realize that it was all an illusion. This world is no more real than the sweet dreams or the nightmares you experience when you are asleep. This reality is just another plane of consciousness that exists along the many other planes.

Reality molds into the unique shape of which you see the world. Our minds are so powerful that they are an activity shaping the world around us at all times. It is very important to understand the power of your mind so that you can be aware of your own responsibility for your life. Your life is fully in the hands of your perception.

If you go to bed at night re-running all the bad things that happened, you will feel like you've had a bad day. If you fall asleep to a movie of what went well about your day, you will feel like you've had a good day. You can experience the same exact thing with the only difference being the way you perceive what happened, and that can change the way you feel.

The Aspiring Alchemist stated that life is like an algorithm. What you focus on is what you are fed more of. Social media uses algorithms to keep people engaged with what they find interesting. If you give a certain topic attention, more of that topic will show up in your feed.

It does not matter if you actually like that topic or not. Your attention will cause more of it to show up in your life. If there is a video that brings you a lot of negative emotion and you comment hateful things on that video, you will see more videos of that same topic on your feed. Algorithms do not decipher between negative or positive attention because it gives you more of what you give your energy to. Life is the same way.

If you focus all of your energy on how angry people are all the time, your life will show you people being angry. You will notice people complaining about the weather or their jobs. Every little complaint will prove your thought to you. Life shows you what you place your energy on. That is why you are the creator of your reality. What you focus your attention on directly manifests into your life.

Mother Teresa was a woman who dedicated her life to helping the poor and the disabled. She won the Nobel Peace Prize for her altruism in 1979. She was a firm believer in spreading peace and justice for all. She did not partake in any anti-war protests but she said, "as soon as you have a pro-peace rally, I'll be there."

The term "anti-war" still has the focus on war. Being anti anything causes that subject to still be holding your attention. Instead of bringing attention to the solution, anti-war protests keep people focused on the problem. Mother Teresa wanted peace not war. She wanted to frame her attention around movement in a positive direction rather than centering it around what was going wrong.

We do not receive what we want; we receive what we are. By tuning to the frequencies of peace and changing your actions to be aligned with those who are peaceful, you will bring more peace into your world. If there is something that you want in this world, focus on it. Be opposed to nothing and for everything. When you are opposed to anything, you are really just perpetuating negative energy. When you support the growth of something, you actively manifest it into your life.

If you are having a hard time dealing with feelings of anger and irritation, do not focus on <u>not</u> being angry. Instead, focus on what you do want. Make the effort to be peaceful and loving. If you tell yourself that you shouldn't be something, that is just another form of rejection of yourself. You have to give yourself something to work towards, not something to work against.

If you have a problem with your weight and overeating, you might consider trying to eat less food. These goals of restriction only make you feel consumed by your weight. Instead of taking something away from yourself, try adding more conscientiousness while you are eating. Focus on what you want, which is a healthy relationship with food. Spend your time eating mindfully, sustaining your health, and loving your body unconditionally.

Do not focus on the problem because that only comes with restrictions and more problems. If your goal is to climb Mount Fitz Roy, you won't reach it by telling yourself to, "stop being lazy." You will reach that goal by telling yourself, "climb Mount Fitz Roy!"

One of the biggest contributors to our quality of lives as individuals is our attitudes. Victor Frankl compared attitude to the last of human freedoms. Our ability to control our attitude is the only thing that can never be taken away from us.

What makes a positive person a positive person is not their quality of life but the way they view their life. Everyone goes through hard shit. There is no such thing as a perfect life. **There is only life and what you make of it.** Each day you have the choice to wake up with a mind that is ready to see the beauty in the struggle or fight against it; the choice is yours.

There are no good or bad experiences. Your mind creates the terms "good" and "bad", "right" and "wrong." This sense of duality is created through our separateness as individuals. In the physical world, there is duality because our mind tells us so. The universe, though, abides by the term, non duality. This means that there is no separation between light and dark, good and bad, yin and yang. They are all a part of the same thing. The good and bad come from the same place of universal consciousness. Duality is the illusion that opposites are separate, and separateness is created through our perception of the world.

If you encounter an experience that hurts you, your mind deems it as a bad experience. Though you may experience pain momentarily, that pain is really just your vehicle to a higher state of consciousness. Everything you experience is leading you closer to a state of pure love and enlightenment.

There is an old Buddhist story about a father and a son who lived on a farm.

The father had a horse that would help him maintain his farm. One day the horse ran away. The people from the village heard about this and gave their condolences to the farmer for his bad luck. The farmer responded, "Forget good, forget bad. It just is."

A few days later, the horse came running back to the farm with six more horses by its side. The people from the village got wind of this. When they went to congratulate him, the farmer responded, "Forget good. Forget bad. It just is."

Several days later, the farmer's son fell off one of the horses while he was riding it in the field. He broke his leg and was crying to his father asking, 'What did I do to deserve this bad luck?'

The farmer carried his son back home and said, "Forget good. Forget bad. It just is."

A few weeks later, a recruiter for the army was coming around the village to recruit young men to fight in the war that just broke out between their country and a neighboring country. When he knocked on the farmer's door, the farmer's son with the broken leg answered. He would not have to fight in the war due to his disability.

Things are constantly happening to us at all times. When we place what we experience into categories of good or bad, we fail to zoom out and see the greater picture. The farmer's indifference shows that things will always happen, neither good nor bad they just do. The way we experience any situation we face is shaped by how we feel about it. You always end up exactly where you need to be. Every situation is just another way the universe is experiencing itself.

It is important to acknowledge that our biology and upbringing can affect how easy it is for us to control our attitudes. Some people struggle with chemical imbalances that make it tougher for them to have a positive outlook on life. While that adds an extra challenge to life, they are not destitute to a life without happiness. At every moment, we can choose to TRY to find the beauty in every given situation. You may not feel it all the time, but you can always try. If you keep trying, one day you won't have to anymore.

I've often found myself being caught in self-pity and victim-hood. It can be addicting to think the world is against you because it is hard to take responsibility for your enjoyment of life. If you admit that life is just your perspective then you can no longer blame your unhappiness on anyone else. This is a hard thing to practice in everyday life. When people say mean things to you, cheat you, lie to you, steal from you, it is so easy to bask in the place where you are a victim. But, you are only a victim to your own mind. Your mind is what separates what happens to you from you. Everything that you experience is leading you to a higher place of consciousness. Every "bad" thing that you go through is helping you grow, helping you become stronger.

There is something so indulgent about feeling bad for ourselves. We desire more than anything to be seen for our scruples. We want people to acknowledge what we've been through and see how hard we've worked. The truth is, nobody can see you but you. That person you are trying to receive validation from is just you.

Other people's sympathy will not make your pain go away. You do not need to prove to anyone how strong you are. You already prove it to yourself when you wake up everyday despite what you've been through. We all just want to be understood, but playing the victim will only make you feel like a victim. Indulging in self-pity only leads you to a place of powerlessness, depression, and emptiness. It is your choice to take everything you experience as an opportunity to make you better.

When you believe that life is working for you, it really starts working for you. Your belief is a direct cause of what you experience. When you feel like a victim and you want to fold into that small, helpless place, remember that you don't actually want that; it just feels familiar. What you actually want is to be happy and peaceful. Your capacity to be happy is only as big as your willingness to take responsibility for your happiness. Being a victim is a choice. Letting your battles make you stronger is also a choice. Responsibility seems hard, but it is harder to be a victim. You have the power. The power of your attitude never leaves your side.

It is not always easy to have a positive outlook on life. We often say that we will try to be more optimistic and then get stuck in our old negative thinking patterns. There are tricks that can help you break old thinking patterns and start embarking on a new positive outlook on life.

One trick is reflection/journaling. Every night before I fall asleep I ask myself these questions:

- What are three things I'm thankful for?
- What are three things I'm proud of myself for?
- How is the Universe showing me it's supporting me?
- What was the highlight of my day?
- What made me smile today?
- What are three things I'm excited for tomorrow?

When I answer these questions before I fall asleep at night, my brain is framed to think about what went well about my day. This trains my subconscious mind to find moments of gratitude throughout my day because I know that I will have to answer these questions at night. Whenever I laugh super hard at any point in the day, my brain reminds me, this is one of the things that made me smile! Or when something serendipitous happens, my brain actively notices how the universe is supporting me.

We actually, believe it or not, experience a lot of joy in our daily lives. This joy so easily gets overridden by thought after thought without conscious awareness of our gratitude. You have probably heard the statistics about what percentage of our thoughts are negative. Research by the National Science Foundation shows that 80% of our thoughts are negative.

This statistic seems ridiculously high and pessimistic, but that is because we don't take the time to embellish our positive thoughts. We have many moments of happiness but they don't register in our brains as potently because they imply that something doesn't need to be fixed. What can our human brains do with happiness? Enjoy it? We are in such a problem oriented society that we often put progress over appreciation. This is not to say that growth and change should not be something you're thinking about, but you must also leave room for gratitude and happiness. Otherwise, what's the point of it all?

When you experience negative thoughts, you are always one angle, one step, one perspective away from thinking positively about it. Another trick that can help you think more positively is to become acutely aware of your negative emotions. Emotions are directly correlated to what you are thinking. There is so much shame behind feeling badly, so we often push these feelings aside and never confront them. This does not cause them to go away. It only causes them to latch onto our brains like a tumor and affect our daily lives. When we confront our emotions, we find out what thought patterns are causing them. You can then face these thought patterns with a lens of positivity. Ask yourself, how can I think about this through the lens of love? How can I think about this through the lens of gratitude? Once you answer those questions, you know what you have to do. It might not be easy to execute the solution right away, but it will become easier and easier the more positively you think.

Thoughts are like possibilities that have no gravitational weight to who you are. You make them possible by believing in them and attaching yourself onto them.

You can let go of any negative thoughts by aligning yourself with your conscious awareness behind that thought. There is a part of you that doesn't think; it just observes your thinking. This part of you is always peaceful because it is your loving awareness. It is that part of you that knows its oneness with everything and knows that it is all right. We forget that this part of us is there because it sits idly by, not interfering with the process of being human, but this part of you is eternal and divine. This part of you is God. When you become aware of this zen place in your mind, you can let go of thoughts and watch them float away like a balloon into space.

We have many desires as humans. We want more money, more time, and more love. We want less stress, less hardship, and less longing. We spend our lives chasing things that we think will bring us more happiness. We want better jobs, bigger houses, a better body, more friends. Have you ever wanted something so badly that you thought all your problems would go away once you received it? And then when you attained that thing, you were happy for a little while until you inevitably went back to wanting something else. The human cycle of desire is one that keeps going round and round. There is always more to have. There is always somewhere better to be. This cycle is exhausting and unfulfilling. When you chase things or experiences, you are always going to be left unfulfilled.

It is an illusion that what we long for can be attained through the external world. What we really crave is the feeling that our desires bring.

We want the emotion of getting what we want, not the actual thing we want.

You may think that a better job will bring you happiness, and it might for a little while, but that happiness won't last because things lose their meaning after time passes. What you really want is to feel appreciated and purposeful in life. You might think that a new job is the answer to your emotional fulfillment, but the only answer is changing your emotions. There is no difference between keeping your same job and attaining happiness than finding a new job and attaining happiness. Happiness is what you want.

When people manifest certain things into their life, they tend to focus too hard on the actual outcome rather than the emotion behind the outcome. True manifestation happens when you tune to the emotion that you want to experience regardless of if you have what you are manifesting. If there is something that you desire, find out what you would feel like if you got that thing. What emotions would it bring you? Then try to feel those emotions in the present moment through the power of your mind. You can use visualization to reach the emotion you want to feel or gratitude for what you already have. Once you reach the emotion that you want to feel, you can let go of the outcome you originally wanted. If it's meant to happen, it will, but it does not matter if it happens or not because you have unlocked the true benefit already.

Our thoughts are actively controlling our lives because we are taught to rationalize everything and think before we act. Thoughts are like pieces of debris flowing down a river.

If you are in a canoe paddling down the river, you watch your thoughts flow by like little twigs and specks of dirt. Sometimes you get caught by big logs because you think they don't belong in the river. As we know, all natural things belong in a river because mother nature makes no mistakes. The thoughts that consume you, thoughts filled with anger, hatred, perversion, violence, embarrassment, these are like the big logs that you might hit while paddling down the river. When you have thoughts that you feel are wrong or don't belong, you are getting too attached to your thinking mind. There are no good or bad thoughts. There are just thoughts that you let pass and ones you latch on to.

You are not defective for having thoughts that make you shameful, scared, angry, or lonely, You are merely a human that does not know how to paddle through the debris in the water. Everything that passes through the river is a natural occurrence. Sometimes the river is filled with dirt, snow, fish, poop, fish poop, but it is all meant to be there because that is nature. The thoughts that run through your mind have no bearing on who you are.

You have a human mind, so you get to experience the act of thinking. Having thoughts and thinking are actually two separate things. Joseph Nguyen explains this well in his book Don't Believe Everything You Think. Nguyen elucidates that thoughts are messages that we will always observe as long as we are in human form, but thinking is an act that we adapt because we are taught to. When you are thinking, you are latching your attention onto your thoughts. Instead of letting your thoughts flow down the river and passing them in the canoe, you stop and collect them. If you collect too many thoughts in your canoe, you will start to sink. This is what happens when we overthink. All negative emotions come from our attachments to our thoughts. But if we allow our conscious awareness to be the focal point of attention, then we can let negative thoughts pass by. Peace is the natural state of being. Any other emotion is a result of the fantasy that our minds convince us is the truth.

Our minds are arguably the most powerful operating systems we get to experience while being in human form. The mind is a gift but only if you know how to use it to your advantage. Remember that your mind does not control you, you control your mind. If you are reading this right now, YOU have the power to create the life you want. You have the power to experience joy and gain strength to conquer all of your mental battles. Each day you have a new opportunity to rewire your thinking patterns and slowly build a more positive attitude towards life. There is no task too big for you to handle, including your happiness.

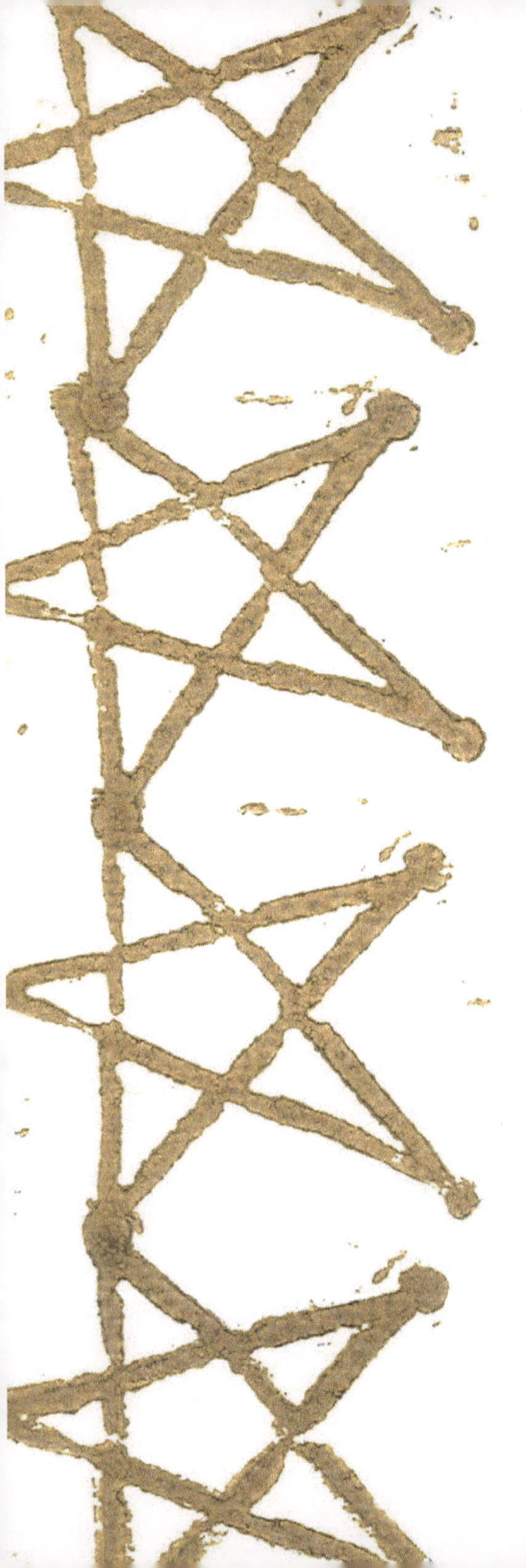

What would be more delusional?

To assume that everything is working out in your favor or to never harness the power of your perspective?

Guided

What we want is not always what is best for us.

A dog begging for chocolate

A hermit longing for a lover

A desert thirsting for rain

A masochist reaching for pain

Desire is the best tasting illusion,

though it will never leave you satisfied.

We are given what we need,

though we may never know why.

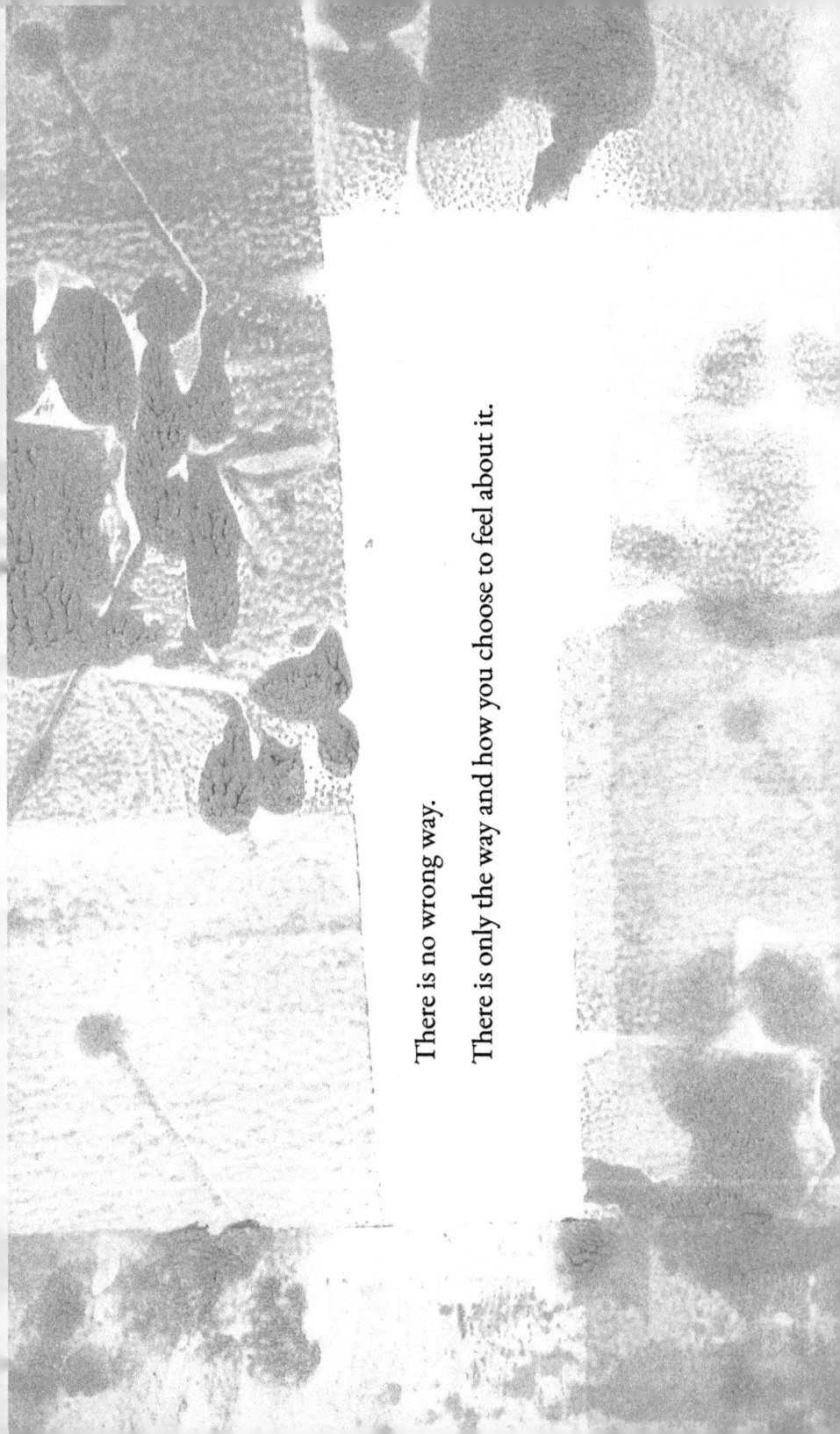

There is no wrong way.

There is only the way and how you choose to feel about it.

WE ARE BIGGER THAN WE THINK

The solar system resides in the pathways of your mind.

This world is as real as the dream you had last night.

You think you are in the world, but the world is within you.

The creation of reality, there's nothing greater you can do.

You are the pillow that supports your head.

You are the loved ones that tucked you into bed.

You created the war to have peace.

You experienced the pain so that you can teach.

You molded the universe into an incarnation to experience the beauty of it all.

Sometimes it takes a unique perspective, and that's why you are small.

The ants crawling in the dirt, the sun, the stars, the earth, are no different from each other.

Everything to exist is just a transformation of you as the divine lover.

Wish for nothing.

Appreciate everything.

Gratitude is a verb that you must act on.

Oh how good it feels not to give into
that negative, cynical part of myself

and realize that it is a

 choice to feel better.

When you let go of expectations,

nothing can go wrong.

Awareness

I see it and let it fly
flutter away
declutter my brain like a clearing in the sky

For I am not the one that sees
or the one that hears
I am not even my breathe
or the eyes that shed tears

You lose me once you name me
The one that perceives cannot be perceived
Just know that I am here
and it is peace from where I am standing

I am unthinkable, yet simple
unintellectual, yet all knowing
formless, yet creator of form
eternal, yet never born

Death

Death is a human construct. Like all human constructs, it is an illusion. Just because it is an illusion doesn't mean that it doesn't come with fear, grief, and sadness. When most people think about death, a cold shiver runs through their body. Death is a taboo subject for most societies because it feels like the ultimate human fear. What could be worse than ceasing to exist forever? What could be worse than never having another chance to finish all the things that you started? As humans, we cannot imagine a worse possible outcome than dying, yet we all inevitably die.

The reason why death is an illusion is because you never belonged to your body in the first place. Most people think that their only identity is the human body that they were incarnated into. Our minds are attached to our bodies because that is all we know ourselves to be. We hear our names called to us all our lives. Our executive functions flow through our nerves. It is hard not to identify with the fingers that you can control or the thoughts that paint pictures in your mind. We believe that our human form is all we are because this is all we know on this physical plane, but you existed long before you had a physical form.

The word "before" is an inaccurate way of describing how long you have existed. Any preposition that I use to share this concept deals with time, but you exist beyond time. The fact of the matter is that you have always just been here. You have always existed in the now, with or without human form because you are existence.

There is nothing without you. When you drop your human form and face what society calls "death", you actually still exist. Your human form is no longer on this physical plane, but your energy cannot be destroyed. You are everything. The illusion is that you were somebody, but your body never belonged to you. It was merely a vessel that you were meant to inhabit for a short period of time. When people die, they claim that they "lost their life", but you cannot lose what never belonged to you. We feel too attached to our physical form, but it is only a tiny speckle of who we are.

You came to this earth to do the work that needed to be done. You are the person that this earth needed at this time. And when your physical form is no longer needed here, when you've been through your karma and helped others through theirs, you will go back to being limitless, to belonging everywhere. Ram Dass has a friend that does not have a physical form. He asked his friend Emmanual what death was like and Emmanual responded, "dying is like taking off a tight shoe." This life is precious; it is beautiful. But it is also hard and filled with pain. Having a physical form requires you to mold into the circumstances of whatever life you were given.

If you're an American, you have to go to school and pay taxes. If you were born into a religious family, you have to go to church as a young child. You have to have a name. You have to feed yourself when you're hungry. You have to make money to buy food, water, and shelter. You have to have a family with whom you share blood. There are many things that are required of humans on this physical plane, but when you die, there are no more rules because there is no more form. When Emmanual compares life to a tight shoe, we get the imagery of life feeling uncomfortable. Life is uncomfortable. It makes us feel limited and small. Your human body is the tight shoe that is holding your eternal spirit. But your spirit does not wear this tight shoe out of obligation. You chose to be exactly where you are in whatever human body you are in. Your human body is a direct servant of the divinity within you.

Death is freedom, not like being let out of jail freedom but like the last day of school freedom. Life is where you learn. You have to work hard to survive here on earth. This whole learning experience of your existence is like the school year. Death is like summer break where you have no rules and your spirit is filled with golden light. Those who try to reach summer break quicker by dropping out of school before the lessons are over, will end up having to do more school in the long-run. Life is your course. It will let go of you when it is ready to. As long as you are still here there is work to be done. You have eternity to be with God on summer break, but right now you are supposed to learn here on earth. There is no wrong place, wrong time. Every birth and every death serves its purpose, no matter the pain it causes people.

There is no doubt that death comes with sorrow, and this is okay. Even the most profound spiritual leaders go through times of grief after losing a loved one. Whatever emotions arise when a death takes place should be dealt with tenderness. Observe your emotions while saying, "I see you. I hear you." All of your feelings are only temporary and they are symptoms of being human.

When you dive deeper, past your human mind into your awareness, you will find the part of you that is not sad. This part of you is just observing the sadness, knowing that it must be felt. The idea of never seeing someone you care about ever again makes us want to rip our hearts out and drown in our agony. The emotions that come with death are some of the most intense endeavors that humans face. To grieve is to have loved.

Once you can see through your pain like a clearing in the fog, you will find that the person you lost is not gone. They are more within everything than they were before. You will see them in a magical sunset. You will hear them in the songs that play on the radio. You will breathe them in through the fumes of their favorite flower. Their human body is longer here, but they were always much more than that. They were pure love, pure divinity. They are the same divinity that is within you. Every time that you tap into your loving awareness, you are meeting them there because that's who we really are.

Every time you close your eyes and listen to your breathing and you let go of attachment and thoughts, you are in the same place that you will be in after you are dead. This place is peaceful. This place is home. Death will bring you back to the familiar place of love that you left to experience physical form on earth. When you die, there is nothing to be afraid of. You are transforming back into the one. You do not have to worry about the people that you are leaving on earth because they will be with you every time they tap into their loving awareness.

It was a part of their karma to experience life on earth with you. It is also a part of their karma to experience life on earth without you.

You will never be separated from anyone for long. Your life is a grain of sand. It is such a tiny fraction of time. When you think about eternity, 100 years is almost nothing in comparison. We have such limited time in our bodies, such limited time in this unique incarnation. Knowing that this will not last forever, only makes each moment here on earth even more precious.

One day you will run for the last time, you will eat your last meal, you will watch your last movie, you will look at yourself one last time in the mirror. One day your human body will disintegrate back into the dirt. You will no longer be able to cry or dance to your favorite songs. Yourself, as you know it, will no longer be. But right now, you are here.

In this exact moment you have the ability to sprint down a grassy hill. You have the ability to make someone smile. You could dunk your head underwater and feel the beads dripping off your skin. The world is yours to embrace. You are alive. You have won the greatest gift and you are experiencing it RIGHT NOW.

Never let life make you forget how great it is. To be a human is to experience something so incredibly raw, so incredibly real. Take each moment to surrender to the beauty. Life will pass you by,even faster than you can blink. But we have this, right here, right now. What are you going to do with it?

What does living mean to you?

Do that.

Me

I'm looking in the mirror.

The peach fuzz on my cheeks is shining in the yellow bedroom light.

The night is soft.

I am enthralled with my pupils,

the same ones that saw the world for the first time.

My body

My face

My smile

My person for this speck of peculiar existence.

Oh how I love seeing the world through these eyes.

Oh how I know this will not last forever.

But oh how I can love being me while I am.

Lay it all out there.

Your dreams, your words, your desires.

Live completely.

What else is there to do?

Awaken

Allow your mortality to drive yourself to live exactly how you want to.

Fear not of death but of wasting your life doing anything other than what is aligned with your soul.

What is life if you never allow yourself to live?

What is death if you live like you're already dead?

This incarnation can no longer sleep in a casket.

I want to breathe in sky.

I want to lay on my back and just be myself for awhile.

There is still time to be.

There is still time.

The cosmos are dancing

through your human body.

Death Therapy

Refuse to be one of those people who needs to feel death around the corner to start living.

The moments of being a human are fleeting.

This is not a trial-run.

This is the one.

The one life you get with your unique interpretation of the world.

You are alive right now.

Don't forget it.

Run.

Feel your feet hit the ground.

Feel the air piercing your lungs.

Wherever you are,

Just be there.

Feel it all.

Don't let a second go by without taking in all it has to offer.

When you die,

all your human achievements wash
away

like a wave flattening out footprints
in the sand.

All that's left is love.

The End

(a transformation into something new)

Dear Readers,

My gratitude extends to all of you for reading this book and applying yourself to be the best person you can be. I know that there is so much light inside of you, and for the sake of yourself and the world, I hope you have the courage to share it. You are beautiful. You are whole. I have endless love for you and you have endless love for you too, even if you are not aware of it.

If you feel called to, it would be wonderful if you could leave a review for this book on Amazon. If not, no biggie :).I would love to hear your honest feedback, kind or critical, just don't make me cry.

You can also reach me at maddierekowski@gmail.com. It would be amazing to hear from any of you about anything you have to say. My Instagram is @maddierekowski where I am relatively active and we can stay connected. My goal is to keep growing in being able to help other people so feedback is always appreciated!

You are doing wonderful. You are living beautifully. Care for yourself gently.

With love,

Maddie

www.ingramcontent.com/pod-product-compliance
Lightning Source LLC
Chambersburg PA
CBHW051157120626
46547CB00012B/1100